REA: THE TEST PREP AP TEACHERS RECOMMEND

AP BIOLOGY
CRASH COURSE

By Michael D'Alessio

Watchung Hills Regional High School
Warren, New Jersey

D1367240

 Research & Education Association
Visit our website at: www.rea.com

Planet Friendly Publishing
✔ Made in the United States
✔ Printed on Recycled Paper
   Text: 10%   Cover: 10%
Learn more: www.greenedition.org

At REA we're committed to producing books in an earth-friendly manner and to helping our customers make greener choices.

Manufacturing books in the United States ensures compliance with strict environmental laws and eliminates the need for international freight shipping, a major contributor to global air pollution.

And printing on recycled paper helps minimize our consumption of trees, water and fossil fuels. This book was printed on paper made with **10% post-consumer waste**. According to Environmental Defense's Paper Calculator, by using this innovative paper instead of conventional papers, we achieved the following environmental benefits:

Trees Saved: 4 • Air Emissions Eliminated: 649 pounds
Water Saved: 638 gallons • Solid Waste Eliminated: 192 pounds

For more information on our environmental practices, please visit us online at **www.rea.com/green**

Research & Education Association
61 Ethel Road West
Piscataway, New Jersey 08854
E-mail: info@rea.com

AP BIOLOGY CRASH COURSE

Copyright © 2011, 2010 by Research & Education Association, Inc. All rights reserved. No part of this book may be reproduced in any form without permission of the publisher.

Printed in the United States of America

Library of Congress Control Number 2010940972

ISBN-13: 978-0-7386-0662-0
ISBN-10: 0-7386-0662-6

REA® is a registered trademark of
Research & Education Association, Inc.

AP BIOLOGY
CRASH COURSE
TABLE of CONTENTS

HEREDITY AND EVOLUTION: HEREDITY, MOLECULAR GENETICS AND EVOLUTIONARY BIOLOGY

PART III

ORGANISMS AND POPULATION: DIVERSITY OF ORGANISMS, STRUCTURE AND FUNCTION OF PLANTS AND ANIMALS, ECOLOGY

PART IV

**PART
V**

THE EXAM

ABOUT THIS BOOK

REA's *AP Biology Crash Course* is the first book of its kind for the last-minute studier or any AP student who wants a quick refresher on the course. The *Crash Course* is based upon a careful analysis of the AP Biology Course Description outline and actual AP test questions.

Written by an AP teacher, our easy-to-read format gives students a crash course in Biology. The targeted review chapters prepare students for the exam by focusing on the important topics tested on the AP Biology exam.

Unlike other test preps, REA's *AP Biology Crash Course* gives you a review specifically focused on what you really need to study in order to ace the exam. The review chapters offer you a concise way to learn all the important facts, terms, and biological processes before the exam.

The introduction discusses the keys for success and shows you strategies to help you build your overall point score. Parts Two, Three, and Four are made up of our review chapters. Each chapter presents the essential information you need to know about Biology.

Part Five focuses exclusively on the format of the AP Biology exam. Each chapter in this section explains a specific aspect of the test, including Major AP Biology Themes and Their Relationship to the Test, the 12 AP Biology Labs, and Essay Writing (exemplars, data analysis/graphing techniques, setting up an experiment).

No matter how or when you prepare for the AP Biology exam, REA's *Crash Course* will show you how to study efficiently and strategically, so you can boost your score!

To check your test readiness for the AP Biology exam, either before or after studying this *Crash Course*, take our **FREE online practice exam**. To access your free practice exam, visit *www.rea.com/crashcourse* and follow the on-screen instructions. This true-to-format test features automatic scoring, detailed explanations of all answers, and will help you identify your strengths and weaknesses so you'll be ready on exam day!

Good luck on your AP Biology exam!

ABOUT OUR AUTHOR

Michael D'Alessio earned his BS in Biology from Seton Hall University, South Orange, New Jersey, and his MS in Biomedical Sciences from the University of Medicine and Dentistry of New Jersey. In 2004, he earned his Executive Master of Arts in Educational Leadership from Seton Hall University.

Mr. D'Alessio has had an extensive career teaching all levels of mathematics and science, including AP Biology, chemistry, physics, algebra and geometry. Most of Mr. D'Alessio's AP Biology students received scores of 4 or 5 on the AP Biology exam.

Currently, Mr. D'Alessio serves as the Supervisor of the Mathematics and Business Department at Watchung Hills Regional High School in Warren, New Jersey, overseeing a department of 30 teachers. In addition, Mr. D'Alessio participates in numerous SAT workshops around the country, preparing students for the mathematics portion of the test.

In 2003, Mr. D'Alessio received the Governor's Teacher of the Year recognition for Watchung Hills Regional High School. In 2004, Mr. D'Alessio received a Certificate of Recognition of Excellence in Science Teaching from Sigma Xi, the Scientific Research Society of Rutgers University and in 2005, he was voted National Honor Society Teacher of the Year by the students of Watchung Hills.

Mr. D'Alessio would like to thank Larry Krieger for encouraging him to write this AP Biology Crash Course and Dr. Jeffrey Charney for his invaluable help in proofreading and editing the manuscript.

ACKNOWLEDGMENTS

In addition to our author, we would like to thank Larry B. Kling, Vice President, Editorial, for his overall guidance, which brought this publication to completion; Pam Weston, Publisher, for setting the quality standards for production integrity and managing the publication to completion; Diane Goldschmidt, Senior Editor, for editorial project management; Alice Leonard, Michael Reynolds, and Kathleen Casey, Senior Editors, for preflight editorial review; Rachel DiMatteo, Graphic Artist, for page design; and Weymouth Design for designing our cover.

We also extend our thanks to Rebekah Warner for technically editing the manuscript, Ellen Gong for proofreading, and Kathy Caratozzolo of Caragraphics for typesetting this edition.

PART I:

INTRODUCTION

Keys for Success on the AP Biology Exam

AP Biology textbooks are very thick and contain thousands of biological facts and concepts. If the AP Biology exam contained all of these facts, the challenge to earn a good score on the exam would be daunting. Studying for this exam requires the student to be a pragmatic learner who can delineate the important tested material from the material that is "interesting to know."

This book will help you become more pragmatic in your studying and streamline your chances to score a 4 or 5 on this exam. The keys to success on the exam include knowing the following:

1. **The Content of the Advanced Placement Biology Examination**

    The Advanced Placement Biology curriculum is based on the content of an introductory biology course taught at the college level. The topics taught in the class reflect major themes that are presented in a number of college-level textbooks. The curriculum of the course also includes 12 thematic-based laboratories. The underpinnings of these labs are based on common biological tenets that are taught in the course. In order to succeed on the exam, students need to master the basic concepts of biology and apply these concepts to various situations in a traditional test format. The make-up of the exam is based on the following percentages in three topics of understanding:

    I.   Molecules and Cells, 25%

    II. Heredity and Evolution, 25%

    III. Organisms and Populations, 50%

The AP Biology examination is 3 hours in length, consisting of an 80-minute, 100 multiple-choice-question section and a 90-minute, free-response section with 4 essays. You are given a 10-minute reading period in which you may read the essay questions and outline a format to respond to the questions.

Part I.   80 minutes, 100 multiple-choice questions = 60% of the grade

The number of multiple-choice questions from each topic is based on the percentages above. For example, expect the following:

> 25 multiple-choice questions pertaining to Molecules and Cells

> 25 multiple-choice questions pertaining to Heredity and Evolution

> 50 multiple-choice questions pertaining to Organisms and Populations

Part II.   90 minutes, 4 essay free-response section = 40% of the grade

> One essay will be from Topic I, Molecules and Cells

> One essay will be from Topic II, Heredity and Evolution

> Two essays will be from Topic III, Organisms and Populations

One or more of these essays could require you to interpret scientific data from one of the 12 required AP laboratories. Each free response is weighted equally, and you must answer them in essay form (outlines are not acceptable).

2.   Process- vs. Content-Based Questions

Content-based questions are simply designed in order to test your ability to know and recall facts about a particular topic. For example, below is a multiple-choice question on cell respiration:

> In cell respiration, glucose is converted to pyruvate in which of the following metabolic pathways?
>
> (A)   Gluconeogenesis
>
> (B)   Krebs cycle

(C) Glycolysis

(D) Light Dependent Reaction

(E) Oxidative Phosphorylation

The correct answer is (C). Glycolysis is a ten-step anaerobic pathway that converts glucose (6 carbon sugar) to 2 pyruvate molecules (3 carbon atoms each).

The good news is that content-based questions make up a good portion of the AP exam. It is essential to know these basic ideas when confronted by this type of question. This book will give you the content you need to know in a *Crash Course* manner.

Process-based questions are designed for you to apply the content you have learned to a situation. You should not be intimidated by these types of questions, because knowing the content goes a long way in helping you determine the correct answer. The questions tend to be in the laboratory/ experimental-based questioning part of the exam. It is crucial for you to know what should have been interpreted and concluded in the 12 AP labs. Below is an example of a process-based question:

A biologist prepares an *in vitro* sample of the activity of the enzyme protease, which promotes the hydrolysis of proteins to amino acids. Three flasks containing 20 milliliters of 5% hemoglobin (a protein) in water are prepared with the addition at time zero of each of the substances indicated in the diagram below.

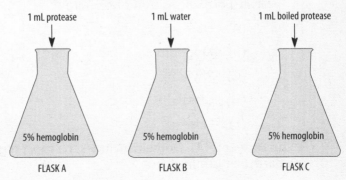

1 mL protease   1 mL water   1 mL boiled protease

5% hemoglobin   5% hemoglobin   5% hemoglobin

FLASK A   FLASK B   FLASK C

In the experiment above, which flask(s) would you expect hemoglobin molecules to maintain a higher-level protein structure?

(A) Flask A

(B) Flask B

(C) Flask C

(D) Flasks A and B

(E) Flasks B and C

The correct answer is (E). Water is the control, and boiled protease will have lost its enzymatic activity because of enzymatic denaturation. The content to apply to correctly answer this process-based question is the definition of a controlled experiment and physical properties of enzymes.

The good news is that process-based questions make up a smaller portion of the AP exam when compared to content-based items. This *Crash Course* will help you know the content needed for making the process-based questions easier to handle.

Expect to see multiple-choice questions in the following formats.

Type I. Traditional multiple-choice questions with choices (A) through (E). There is only one correct answer!

Which of the following is MOST inclusive when classifying organisms using taxonomy?

(A) Domain

(B) Kingdom

(C) Phylum

(D) Class

(E) Order

The answer is (A). Domain includes the most organisms within a particular group.

Type II. Heading multiple-choice questions with choices (A) through (E). There is only one correct answer for each question. However, the answers could be used in a set of questions once, more than once, or not at all.

Questions 70–74

   (A)   Immune System

   (B)   Nervous System

   (C)   Digestive System

   (D)   Circulatory System

   (E)   Excretory System

70.   Involves blood that is oxygenated

71.   Enzyme called amylase is an important part of this system

72.   Involved in allergic attacks

73.   Basic unit is called the nephron

74.   Peristalsis is a key type of action

Answers

70. D   71. C   72. A   73. E   74. C

3. How Is the Test Scored?

Section I.   Total scores on the multiple-choice section of the exam are based on the number of questions answered correctly. Points are not deducted for incorrect answers and no points are awarded for unanswered questions.

Multiple-Choice Raw Score

Number Right × .90 = _____

Weighted Score

for Section I

Section II. The free-response section is scored by multiplying the number of raw points earned on each essay by 1.50.

Free-Response Question 1   _____ × 1.50 = _____
(possible points
out of 10)

Free-Response Question 2   _____ × 1.50 = _____
(possible points
out of 10)

Free-Response Question 3   _____ × 1.50 = _____
(possible points
out of 10)

Free-Response Question 4   _____ × 1.50 = _____
(possible points
out of 10)

Combined Free-Response Score   = _____

Composite Score = (MC Weighted Score)
         + (Combined Free-Response Score)

Composite Score Range*	AP Grade
95–150	5
81–94	4
69–80	3
58–68	2
0–57	1

* From the 2009 released exam. Composite score
ranges change year to year.

On the low end you can score 95 out of a possible 150 points (63%) and STILL earn a 5 on the test. To earn a 4 you need 81 points out of a possible 150, or just 54%!!!! This *Crash Course* will help you achieve the highest grade possible on this test.

4. **What Is the Breakdown of AP Biology Grades Across the United States?**

Year	% of Students Earning Examination Grade of				
	5	4	3	2	1
2006	19.6%	20.3%	21.2%	23.3%	15.6%
2007	19.3%	20.3%	21.2%	23.2%	15.9%
2008	18.6%	15.6%	16.1%	15.2%	34.6%

(Data obtained from College Board Student Grade Distribution Reports, 2006–2008.)

The data above indicates that about one out of five of the students who take the AP Biology Examination earned a 5, with a staggering 34.6% of students earning a 1 in 2008. In 2008, there were 154,000 test takers for AP Biology, which was an all-time high. This *Crash Course* is tailored for all of the students represented in the data and will help you earn a grade that will allow you to receive college credit for biology.

5. **Using College Board and REA Materials to Supplement Your *Crash Course***

Your *Crash Course* contains everything you need to know to score a 4 or 5. You should, however, supplement it with materials provided by the College Board and other resources. The AP Biology Course Description Booklet, and the 1999, 2002, and 2008 released AP Biology exams, can all be ordered from the College Board's Online Store (http://store.collegeboard.com). In addition, the College Board's AP Central site (*http://apcentral. collegeboard.com*) contains a wealth of materials, including essay questions with exemplars and rubrics. And finally, REA's *AP Biology (7th Edition)* contains excellent narrative chapters that supplement this *Crash Course* material.

PART II:

MOLECULES AND CELLS: Chemistry of Life, Cells, and Cellular Energetics

Water

I. Chemistry of Life—Water

A. The Amazing Properties of the Water Molecule

1. Water is a *polar molecule*; this means it is a molecule whose ends have opposite charges (hydrogen being positive and oxygen being negative).
2. *Hydrogen bonding*—the ability of hydrogen to interact with the elements fluorine, oxygen, and nitrogen. This is not a covalent bond.
3. For every 1 water molecule, 4 more molecules can hydrogen-bond with the original.
4. Most abundant molecule in living organisms.
5. Water exhibits hydrogen bonding leading to the following properties.
   i. *Cohesion*—the ability of water molecules to stick together. Example: the movement of water against gravity on plant surfaces.
   ii. *Adhesion*—the ability of water to adhere to molecules other than water. Example: water moving through a hose and adhering to the inside of the hose.
   iii. *Surface Tension*—the measure of how difficult it is to break the surface of water. Example: the high surface tension of water allows a water strider (skater) to walk on the surface of a pond with minimal effort.
   iv. *Specific Heat*—the amount of energy (heat) it takes to raise or lower the temperature of one gram of a substance 1 degree Celsius. Water has a high specific heat; therefore, large bodies of water do not evaporate easily.

v. *Evaporative Cooling*—since water has a high heat of vaporization, once water leaves a surface, the surface cools down. Example: the sweat of an athlete assists in maintaining homeostasis during a vigorous workout.

B. Dissociation of Water (or the shifting of hydrogen from one water molecule to another)
   1. $2H_2O \leftrightarrow H_3O^+$ (hydronium ion) + OH^- (hydroxide ion)
   2. The counterbalance of hydronium and hydroxide results with a pH of 7.0 for water.
   3. *Acid* (biological definition)—a molecule that increases hydronium concentration.
      Example: $HCl \rightarrow H^+ + Cl^-$
   4. *Base* (biological definition)—a molecule that increases hydroxide concentration.
      Example: $NaOH \rightarrow Na^+ + OH^-$
   5. pH scale—ranges from 0–14, with 7 being neutral. Each increment of 1 on the pH scale is a ten-fold change.
   6. The deleterious effects of acid rain—production of carbon dioxide and sulfur oxides from industrial manufacturing leads to the production of acidic conditions (H_2CO_3 and H_2SO_4). Acid rain affects ecosystems such as lakes and forests.

Test Tip

Molecules and Cells—*Inquiry about the amazing properties of water has been expanded in AP Biology essays. Water is a recurring theme found in all aspects of molecules and cells.*

Organic Molecules in Organisms

I. Chemistry of Life—Organic Molecules in Organisms

A. *Organic Chemistry*—the study of carbon-containing compounds

1. Carbon is the building block of the four major macromolecules: carbohydrates, lipids, proteins, and nucleic acids.

2. *Tetra-valence* or the ability to form 4 covalent bonds is a hallmark of the carbon atom.

B. *Functional Groups*—groups of accessory elements that attach to molecules that give them a *different structure, and thus a different function*

1. *Hydroxyl Group*—hydrogen bonded to oxygen attached to a carbon skeleton. Molecules with hydroxyl groups are considered *alcohols*.

—OH
HYDROXYL

2. *Carbonyl Group*—carbon joined to oxygen via a double bond. If the carbonyl group is on the end of a carbon skeleton, it is called an *aldehyde*; otherwise the compound is called a *ketone*.

ALDEHYDE   KETONE

3. *Carboxyl Group*—carbon is doubled bonded to an oxygen and a hydroxyl (*carboxyl* is a combination of carbonyl and hydroxyl)

CARBOXYLIC ACID

4. *Amino Group*—a nitrogen atom bonded to two hydrogen atoms and one carbon. *Amines* are organic molecules that contain an amino group.

$$-NH_2$$

AMINO

5. *Phosphate Group*—a phosphate ion covalently attached to a carbon skeleton. Phosphate groups have a tremendous amount of energy associated with them.

$$O^- $$
$$\|$$
$$O^- —P—O^-$$
$$\|$$
$$O^-$$

PHOSPHATE

C. Biologically Important Molecules

1. *Macromolecules*—large molecules that fall into four categories: carbohydrates, lipids, proteins, and nucleic acids (see the molecular genetics chapter).

2. *Polymer*—a long molecule consisting of similar molecules held together by covalent bonds. *(Poly = many)*

3. *Monomers*—the repetitive molecules of a polymer. *(Mono = one)*

4. The synthesis of polymers takes place through a reaction called *dehydration synthesis (condensation reaction)*. In this reaction *water is lost.*

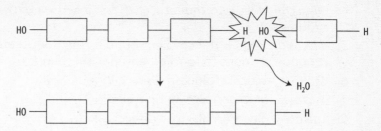

5. The breakdown of polymers takes place through a reaction called *hydrolysis*. In this reaction *water is added across the covalent bond. (Hydro = water, lysis = break)*

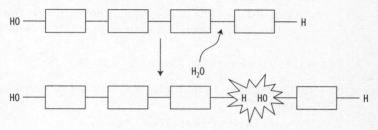

D. Carbohydrates

1. Definition: sugar and the polymers of sugar. Ending with suffix *–ose*. 45–65% of dietary allowance. 4 calories per gram. Excess carbohydrates can be converted to fat.

2. *Monosaccharide*—single sugars with a formula of CH_2O.

3. Most important monosaccharide is glucose. $C_6H_{12}O_6$.

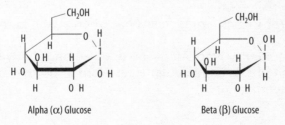

Alpha (α) Glucose   Beta (β) Glucose

Difference is hydroxyl on carbon 1.

4. *Disaccharides*—two monosaccharides linked via dehydration synthesis.
5. *Glycosidic bond* is the covalent bond formed between monosaccharides to form di- and polysaccharides.
6. *Maltose*—glucose/glucose disaccharide.
7. *Sucrose*—glucose/fructose disaccharide.
8. *Lactose*—glucose/galactose disaccharide.
9. *Polysaccharides*—macromolecules with 100–1000 of monomer subunits.
    i. *Storage Polysaccharide*—starch for plants. Glycogen for animals.
    ii. *Structural Polysaccharide*—cellulose for plants (indigestible for humans). Chitin found in arthropods and fungi.

E. Lipids (Fats/Triglycerides, Phospholipids, Steroids)

1. The *only* class of large molecules that are not considered polymers.
2. Lipids are hydrophobic—*fear of water*.
3. Used for insulation and buoyancy in marine and Arctic animals.
4. Major component of membranes.
5. *Fat or triglyceride*—glycerol and 3 fatty acids.
    i. 9 Calories per gram, thus making it the most energy rich of the biologically important compounds. 10–35% of dietary allowance.
    ii. Too much fat causes a build-up in the arteries called *atherosclerosis*.
    iii. *Fatty Acids*—long chains of carbon attached to a carboxyl group.
    iv. *Saturated Fatty Acids*—no double bonds between carbon atoms. Example: Animal fat—lard or butter (solids at room temperature).

v. *Unsaturated Fatty Acid*—has some double bonds between carbon atoms. Example: Plant and fish fat and many vegetable oils (liquids at room temperature).

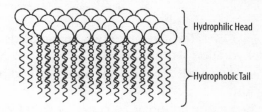

6. *Phospholipids*—are lipids but unlike triglycerides only have 2 fatty acids.
   i. Glycerol + phosphate + 2 fatty acids = *a phospholipid*.
   ii. Head region contains the glycerol and phosphate and is hydrophilic (attracted to water).
   iii. Tail region contains the fatty acids (1 saturated and 1 unsaturated) and is hydrophobic.
   iv. Phospholipids are the basic units of biological membranes.

Hydrophilic Head

Hydrophobic Tail

7. *Steroids*—lipids that consist of 4 fused rings.
   i. Structure of the precursor lipid cholesterol.

H$_3$C

CH$_3$

H$_3$C

CH$_3$

CH$_3$

HO

   ii. Many steroid hormones in animals are produced from cholesterol.

F. Proteins

1. Molecules that perform structural, catalytic, signaling, defense, and transport duties within the cell. Make up about 50% of the dry weight of a cell. 4 calories per gram. 10–35% of dietary allowance.

2. Proteins are made up of monomer units called *amino acids.* An amino acid consists of an amino group, a carboxyl group, and up to 20 different side chain groups (20 different amino acids) that give each amino acid unique physical and chemical properties (*different structure, thus a different function*).

$$H_2N - \underset{\underset{R}{|}}{\overset{\overset{H}{|}}{C}} - \overset{\overset{O}{||}}{C} - OH \qquad R = \text{side chain}$$

3. *Dipeptide* is formed when two amino acids are linked via dehydration synthesis.

4. *Peptide bond* is the covalent bond formed between amino acids.

5. When many amino acids come together via dehydration synthesis, a polypeptide is formed. Polymers of amino acids are called polypeptides, and when one or more polypeptides fold in specific conformations, a protein is formed.

6. A protein conformation (shape) depends on 4 levels of organization.
   i. *Primary Structure*—unique sequence of amino acids.
   ii. *Secondary Structure*—the interaction of hydrogen bonds along the peptide chain forming an alpha (α) helix or beta (β) pleated sheet.
   iii. *Tertiary Structure*—the interaction between the α helix and β pleated sheet. Disulfide bridges, hydrophobic interaction, hydrogen bonding, and Van der Waals forces allow the structure to form.
   iv. *Quaternary Structure*—the interaction of 2 or more polypeptide chains forming a multi-subunit protein. Examples include DNA polymerase, collagen, and hemoglobin.

v. *Denaturation*—an inactive form of a protein (back to primary sequence) can take place with changes to pH, salt concentration, temperature, or exposure to toxic compounds.

7. *Protein homology*—refers to the fact that certain proteins have similar structures that are found in more than one species that share a common ancestor. These proteins share a high degree of amino acid correspondence. An example is the cytochrome c protein found in the electron transport chain. The data below indicates humans and rhesus monkeys are closer on the evolutionary chain than humans and tuna.

Species	Number of Amino Acid Differences When Compared to Humans
Human	0
Rhesus monkey	1
Kangaroo	10
Snapping turtle	15
Bullfrog	18
Tuna	21

Test Tip

Molecules and Cells—*Biologically important molecules are great examples of the "structure and function" theme. Be sure to use these examples in essay questions to gain critical points.*

Free Energy Changes

I. Chemistry of Life—Free Energy Changes

A. *Metabolism*—the totality of all chemical reactions that occur within an organism.

B. *Anabolic Reactions*—sets of reactions that consume energy to make molecules. For example, the synthesis of DNA or protein is anabolic.

C. *Catabolic Reactions*—sets of reactions that produce energy in the breakdown of molecules. For example, the breakdown of glucose into carbon dioxide and water with the production of ATP.

D. *Energy*—capacity to do work.

E. *1st law of thermodynamics*—energy can neither be created nor destroyed but can change from one form to another. Example: Plants convert light energy from the sun to make chemical energy in the form of glucose.

F. *2nd law of thermodynamics*—every energy transfer increases the entropy of the universe (disorder).

G. *Free Energy*—the total amount of energy in a system (a cell) that can be tapped to do work. Not all energy transfers are 100%.

H. *Exergonic Reaction*—a reaction that produces a net release of free energy.

   AB → A + B + Energy

I. *Endergonic Reaction*—a reaction that absorbs free energy from its surroundings.

$$A + B + Energy \rightarrow AB$$

J. *Energy Coupling*—using the products of an exergonic reaction to help run an endergonic reaction. The molecule that is essential for coupling of reactions and cellular work is adenosine triphosphate (ATP).

When the terminal (last) bond of phosphate of ATP is broken (via hydrolysis), energy is released (exergonic). Adenosine diphosphate (ADP) is formed.

Hydrolysis of ATP

The ATP cycle is the process in which ATP is hydrolyzed and ADP is *phosphorylated* (addition of a phosphate group) to reform ATP.

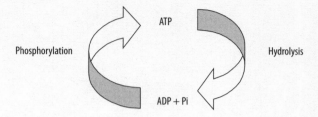

Phosphorylation

ATP

Hydrolysis

ADP + Pi

Molecules and Cells—*ATP is used in a plethora of biological situations including active transport, muscle movement, DNA replication, and cell respiration/photosynthesis.*

Enzymes

I. Chemistry of Life—Enzymes

A. 99.9% of enzymes are proteins in structure. 0.1% are ribozymes made of RNA (found in rRNA).

B. *Enzymes are catalysts* or biological chemical agents that speed up a reaction without being consumed or produced by the reaction. Most enzymes end with the suffix *–ase*.

C. An enzyme works by lowering the activation energy (E_A) of a reaction. *Activation energy* is defined as the amount of input energy needed to start a chemical reaction.

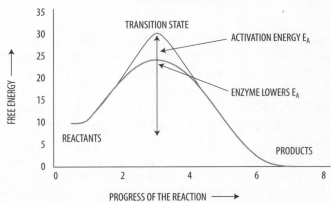

ENERGY PROFILE FOR ENZYME

D. The enzyme combines with the substrate or molecule that the enzyme will work on. When the enzyme and substrate are joined, a catalytic reaction takes place, forming a product. The enzyme can be recycled and used for later reactions.

E. *Active site* of the enzyme is the region that the substrate binds.

F. The catalytic cycle of an enzyme:

Enzyme + Substrate ⟷ Enzyme − Substrate Complex ⟷ Enzyme + Product

Induced Fit Model of Catalysis—the enzyme's active site and substrate bind to each other, "inducing" a very slight change in the structure of the enzyme, which promotes the reaction.

G. Environmental factors that disrupt the activity of enzymes include:

1. Each enzyme has an optimal temperature. If the temperature is too high, the enzyme will *denature* (3-D shape will be lost). If the temperature is too low, the enzyme will slow down.
2. Each enzyme has an optimal pH. If the pH is too high or too low, the enzyme will denature.
3. *Cofactor*—non-organic molecules that augment enzyme activity. Examples: iron, magnesium, and copper.
4. *Coenzyme*—organic molecule that augments enzyme activity. Example: vitamins

H. *Allosteric Site and Regulation*—a portion of the enzyme in which a regulator will bind. This is not the same as the active site. The effect on the enzyme may be stimulatory or inhibitory.

I. *Feedback Inhibition*—when the end product of a biological pathway inhibits the activity of an enzyme involved in that pathway.

J. *Cooperativity*—different from allosteric regulation because the enzyme contains multiple subunits. When a regulator binds to one subunit, the other subunits "follow course" and a conformational change in the enzyme's shape takes place. This has the effect of amplifying the activity of the enzyme.

IMPORTANT ENZYMES TO KNOW

Enzyme	Substrate	Action
Lipase	Lipids	Breaks down lipids
Protease	Proteins	Breaks down protein
DNAse	DNA	Breaks down DNA
RNAse	RNA	Breaks down RNA
Kinase	Any molecule	Transfers phosphate groups
Carboxylase	Any molecule	Adds carbon dioxide to create an additional –COOH group
Decarboxylase	Any molecule	Removes carbon dioxide
Dehydrogenase	Any molecule	Adds electrons and hydrogen

Test Tip

Molecules and Cells—*Knowing a list of enzymes and their substrates is helpful in AP essays. Correctly naming an enzyme and its substrate will translate to points on your essay.*

Prokaryotic and Eukaryotic Cells

I. Cells—Prokaryotic and Eukaryotic Cells

A. Cytology—*"cyto" meaning cell, "logy" meaning study of*—is the branch of biology that studies the structure and function of cells. Microscopes are the instruments that allow the study of the structure of a cell.

1. *Light Microscope*—based on light passing through a two-lens system. Ocular lenses = 10x magnification, objectives lenses = 4x, 10x, 40x, or 100x magnification. Total magnification = ocular × objective. Can view prokaryotic and eukaryotic cells from the light microscope, but not a virus.

2. *Magnification*—ability to enlarge the image.

3. *Resolution*—ability to provide clarity to the image.

4. *Electron Microscope*—uses a beam of electrons to provide greater magnification and resolution.
   i. *Transmission Electron Microscope*—used to view the internal components of cells (organelles).
   ii. *Scanning Electron Microscope*—used to view the surface of cells.

5. *Cell Fractionation* is the ability to use centrifuges (ultracentrifuges) to spin at different high speeds to "fractionate" (split apart) cells.
   i. Homogenate (tear apart)—2 layers (pellet and supernatant) → supernatant contains mitochondria and/or chloroplasts → supernatant contains cell membrane and internal membranes → supernatant contains ribosomes.

B. *Prokaryotic Cell*—unicellular bacteria.

1. Have no nucleus!!!

2. Generally considered the first form of life and were most likely anaerobic.

3. *Nucleoid region*—"devoid" of a true nucleus, but had DNA floating in the cytoplasm. No nuclear membrane.
4. *Cytoplasm*—region between the nucleus and the plasma membrane.
5. *Cytosol*—semi-fluid within the cell.
6. Generally 1 to 10 micrometers in size.
7. Have a *cell membrane*—regulates transport and is very selective in permeability.
8. Have a *cell wall*—protective layer external to the cell membrane. The cell wall does not contain phospholipids or transmembrane proteins.
9. Contains *ribosomes*—location of protein synthesis.
10. *Capsule*—lies outside of the cell wall, made of carbohydrate, and is pathogenic (disease causing).

C. *Eukaryotic Cell*—animal cell or plant cell; members are all multicellular. There are unicellular eukaryotic cells (fungi).

1. Does contain a nucleus.
2. *Nuclear envelope*—double membrane made of phospholipids and proteins. Maximum protection of the DNA in the nucleus.
3. *Nuclear pores*—holes in the envelope that allow transport into and out of the nucleus.
4. *Nuclear lamina*—set of proteins that give the nucleus structure.
5. *Chromatin*—DNA and proteins combine within the nucleus. Coiled DNA around proteins allows maximum occupancy of the nucleus by DNA.
6. *Chromosomes*—coiled chromatin that contains genes.
7. *Nucleolus*—inside the nucleus and the location of where ribosomes are synthesized. Stains dark using cell-staining procedures.
8. *Ribosomes*—found outside of the nucleus and are the location of the synthesis of proteins. (Common between both prokaryotes and eukaryotes.)

Organelles Found in Animal Cells but Not in Plant Cells	Organelles Found in Plant Cells but Not in Animal Cells
Centrioles	Cell Wall
Lysosomes	Chloroplast
Cilia	Central Vacuole
Flagella	Plasmodesmata
Intermediate Filaments	

Test Tip

Molecules and Cells—*Don't be surprised if you are asked to identify the major parts and organelles of a eukaryotic or plant cell. Know all the structures and their locations within the cell. This is a very common question on the AP Biology test. Use your textbook to help you match the location of each structure.*

Membranes

I. Cells—Membranes

A. Made of phospholipids or *amphipathic* molecules—having both hydrophilic (*love water*) and hydrophobic (*hate water*) regions.

B. *Fluid Mosaic Model of Membranes*—the membrane is a mosaic of proteins that are embedded in or attached to the phospholipids.

C. Membranes are not static. The phospholipids within the membrane move laterally, but NEVER flip-flop because the hydrophilic and hydrophobic parts would have to mix. Too much energy is required to flip membranes.

D. *Cholesterol* is found in membranes and helps to make the membrane less fluid. Cholesterol does lower the temperature required to make the membrane solid (needs to be colder because phospholipid molecules cannot pack together).

E. *Integral Proteins*—transmembrane proteins with hydrophobic and hydrophilic portions.

F. *Peripheral Proteins*—bind to the integral proteins on the outside of the cell membrane.

G. *Functions of membrane proteins*
   1. Transport
   2. Enzymatic Activity
   3. Signal Transduction and Cell Communication

4. Cell-to-Cell Contact and Attachment

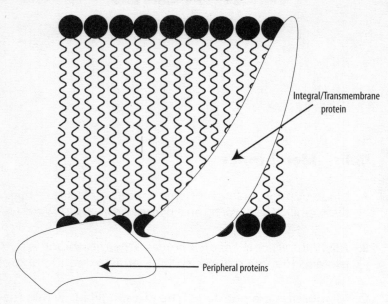

Integral/Transmembrane protein

Peripheral proteins

II. Membrane Trafficking

A. Small molecules that are hydrophobic and nonpolar molecules such as O_2 and CO_2 can cross the membrane with relative ease.

B. Large molecules and charged molecules undergo selective permeability with respect to the membrane.

C. *Transport Proteins*—proteins that aid in moving molecules across the membrane.

D. *Passive Transport or Diffusion*

1. Tendency for molecules to move from a higher concentration to a lower concentration. This type of movement does not require energy (ATP).

2. Substance in diffusion will move down the concentration gradient.
3. *Passive transport*—diffusion across a biological membrane.

E. *Osmosis*

1. Diffusion of water across a selectively permeable membrane. Osmosis *always* takes place from hypotonic to hypertonic.
   i. *Hypertonic*—solution with higher solute concentration.
   ii. *Hypotonic*—solution with lower solute concentration.
   iii. *Isotonic*—solution with equal solute concentration.

Hypertonic Solution	Hypotonic Solution	Isotonic Solution
If you place an animal cell in this type of solution, water will diffuse out of the cell. The cell will be shriveled.	If you place an animal cell in this type of solution, water will diffuse into the cell. The cell will burst or lyse.	If you place an animal cell in this type of solution, water will diffuse in and out of the cell at the same rate. The cell will look normal.
If you place a plant cell in this type of solution, water will diffuse out of the cell. The cell will be plasmolyzed.	If you place a plant cell in this type of solution, water will diffuse into the cell. The cell will be turgid, which for a plant cell is considered normal.	If you place a plant cell in this type of solution, water will diffuse in and out of the cell. The cell will be flaccid.

F. *Facilitated Diffusion*

1. Movement of molecules (usually polar) across the membrane with the aid of membrane transport proteins.
2. This is a type of passive transport, so no energy is used.

G. *Active Transport*

   1. Movement against the concentration gradient; therefore, it requires energy (ATP).
   2. Specific membrane proteins are used in active transport.

H. Other Types of Movement

   1. *Cotransport*—coupling of the movement of molecules into and out of the cell at the same time.
   2. *Exocytosis*—fusion of vesicles and molecules with the plasma membrane. Secretes materials to the outside of the cell.
   3. *Endocytosis*—the cell takes in molecules via vesicles which fuse with the plasma membrane.
   4. *Phagocytosis*—cell engulfs molecules. Most commonly involved in the immune response.
   5. *Pinocytosis*—cellular drinking, or the taking in of fluids in tiny vesicles.
   6. *Receptor-mediated endocytosis*—specific sites on the membrane bind to specific molecules on the outside and engulf them into the cell.

Test Tip

Molecules and Cells—*Don't confuse yourself with plant and animal cells and their conditions in various types of solutions. This is a classic trap question that is intended to confuse the test taker.*

Subcellular Organization

Cells—Subcellular Organization

A. *Endomembrane System*—the different membranes that are within the cytoplasm of a eukaryotic cell. These membranes divide the cell into compartments, or organelles.

1. *Endoplasmic Reticulum (ER)*
    i. Continuous with the nuclear envelope.
    ii. *Smooth ER*—lacks ribosomes. Synthesis of lipids and carbohydrates, detoxification of drugs. High abundance of smooth ER exist in liver cells for the storage of sugar (glycogen) and detoxification. *This is why the liver is the most important organ in the body.*
    iii. *Rough ER*—contains ribosomes. Synthesis of proteins (translation) and new membranes. Site of the convergence of mRNA, tRNA, and rRNA.

2. *Golgi Apparatus*
    i. The global shipping and manufacturing area of the cell.
    ii. Modification of molecules such as proteins takes place.
    iii. Secretion of proteins to other parts of the cell or other cells.
    iv. Synthesis of carbohydrates.

3. *Lysosome*
    i. Contains hydrolytic enzymes that break down macromolecules.
    ii. Enzymes in the lysosome work best at a low pH range.
    iii. Aid in phagocytosis and intracellular digestion.

4. *Vacuoles*
    i. *Food vacuoles*—store broken-down macromolecules.

ii. *Contractile vacuoles*—found in protists and release water, an organelle that contracts and expands.

iii. *Central vacuoles*—found in plant cells and store water, allowing the cell to maintain turgor pressure (pressure on the cell wall). Tonoplasts are the membranes of central vacuoles.

5. *Mitochondria*
   i. Powerhouse of the cell that produces ATP.
   ii. Directly requires oxygen.
   iii. Once thought to be free-living prokaryotes because this organelle has its own DNA that shows a high degree of homology to prokaryotic DNA. DNA is circular, which corresponds to the shape of bacterial DNA.
   iv. Enclosed in an envelope of two membranes.
   v. The inner membrane is folded into internal components called *cristae*. This creates the spaces within the mitochondria called the intermembrane space and mitochondrial matrix.
   vi. Inheritance is always from mother to child.

6. *Chloroplasts*
   i. The chloroplast is separated by two membranes.
   ii. Inside the chloroplast are membranous sacs called *thylakoids*; stacks of thylakoids are called *grana* (singular *granum*).
   iii. Fluid outside of the grana is called *stroma*.
   iv. Can produce ATP (similar to mitochondria) via the light-dependent reaction in photosynthesis.

7. *Peroxisome*
   i. Membrane-bound organelle that transfers hydrogen from compounds to produce hydrogen peroxide.
   ii. The hydrogen peroxide is then converted to water by the enzyme catalase.

8. *Cytoskeleton*—an array of fibers (mostly protein) that span the entire cell, giving it mechanical support and shape. Three main types of fibers: microtubules, microfilaments, and intermediate filaments.
   i. *Microtubules*—made of alpha and beta tubulin protein. Also involved in mitosis.
   ii. *Centrosome*—organelle near the nucleus that produces microtubules.

iii. *Centrioles*—derived from the centrosome and contain a set of microtubules that are composed of nine sets of triplet microtubules. This arrangement is called 9+3. Involved in cell division.

iv. *Cilia and Flagella*—appendages on cells that allow for motility. Cilia increase the surface area of cells and occur in large numbers. Flagella are long tail-like structures that propel movement via undulating motion. Both are composed of nine sets of doublet microtubules. The arrangement is called 9 + 2.

v. *Microfilaments*—made of actin protein.
  • Actin filaments combine with a protein called myosin to allow for muscle movement.
  • *Pseudopodia*—common in amoeboid movement; an extension of the myosin protein via cytoplasmic streaming mimics a foot-like structure.

vi. *Intermediate Filaments*—made of keratin protein.
  • Reinforce cell's shape.
  • Positions organelles in the proper place within the cell.

9. *Cell Surfaces and Junction*
  i. *Extracellular Matrix*—made of glycoproteins (proteins with sugars attached to them) and/or proteoglycans (protein extremely rich in carbohydrates). Aids in communication of cells and cell-to-cell adherence.
  ii. Major glycoprotein in extracellular matrix is collagen.
  iii. Positions organelles in the proper place within the cell.

Cell Cycle and Regulation

I. Cells—Cell Cycle and Its Regulation

A. *Genome*—a cell's total genetic make-up.

B. *Chromosome*—organized structure of DNA that is made up of genes. Eukaryotic chromosomes are linear in structure.

C. *Chromatin*—DNA-protein complex that helps to condense the genetic material into the nucleus of a eukaryotic cell.

D. *Sister Chromatids*—consist of two duplicated chromosomes held together at the centromere.

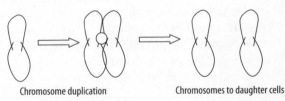

Chromosome duplication   Chromosomes to daughter cells

E. *Mitosis*—one part of the cell cycle, and the process in which a eukaryotic cell divides its nucleus followed by cytokinesis. The end result is two genetically identical cells.

F. *Binary Fission*—cell division in prokaryotes in which the cells are split into two. Prokaryotes have one double-stranded, circular DNA molecule.

G. *Mitotic Cell Cycle*

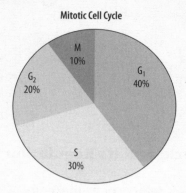

Mitotic Cell Cycle

1. *Interphase*—roughly 90% of the cell cycle and consists of G$_1$, S, and G$_2$. For mammalian cycles, this is roughly 24 hours.
2. *G$_1$ phase*—first gap or portion of cell cycle production of proteins and organelles. Preparation for cell division.
3. *S phase*—DNA synthesis/replication
4. *G$_2$ phase*—second gap or portion of cell cycle production of proteins and organelles. Preparation for cell division.
5. *M phase*—mitosis (4 part process of cell division).

   Prophase
   i. Fragmentation of nuclear membrane.
   ii. Chromatin condenses together into chromosomes.
   iii. The duplicated chromosomes have two sister chromatids bound together at the centromere.
   iv. Formation of the mitotic spindle fiber.

   Metaphase
   i. Microtubules attach to kinetochores or proteins on the chromosomes where the mitotic spindle attaches.
   ii. Chromosomes line up on metaphase plate.

   Anaphase
   i. Separation of sister chromatids.
   ii. Breakdown of the microtubules forces the sisters to opposite poles.

   Telophase
   i. Sometimes called reverse prophase.
   ii. Nuclear envelope starts to form.

      iii. Chromosomes are now surrounded by new nuclear
envelope and unfold back into chromatin. Mitosis is
complete, *cell division is not.*

Cytokinesis

      i. Separate process, and not part of mitosis, in which
daughter cells are formed with identical genetic material.

      ii. Animal cells form a *cleavage furrow* that separates into two
cells.

      iii. Plant cells form a *cell plate* that separates into two cells.

H. *Regulation of Cell Cycle*

  1. *Checkpoints*—essential points during the cell cycle that
regulate the process of passing from one stage to the next.

  2. G_o—a non-dividing stage of the cell cycle that halts the cycle
from proceeding.

  3. *Growth Factor*—protein/hormone that promotes the division
of cells.

  4. *Density-dependent Inhibition*—process in which cells stop
dividing when they are in contact with each other.

  5. *Anchorage Dependence*—Cells must be attached to something
in order to divide properly.

  6. *Cancer Cell*—cells that are said to be "transformed" from
normal cells to cancer cells and do not exhibit density-
dependent inhibition. Have uncontrolled growth pattern.

  7. *Tumor*—a pocket of abnormal cells amongst normal cells.

  8. *Benign tumor*—non-spreading of abnormal cells.

  9. *Malignant tumor*—abnormal cells that invade and impact the
normal function of an organ.

  10. *Metastasis*—spreading of malignant tumor to other parts of
the body.

Coupled Reactions

I. Cellular Energetics—Coupled Reactions

A. *Coupled Reactions*—a chemical reaction having a common intermediate in which energy is transferred from one reaction to another.

B. The processes of cellular respiration and photosynthesis are coupled to each other. The products of one reaction end up being the reactants in the other.

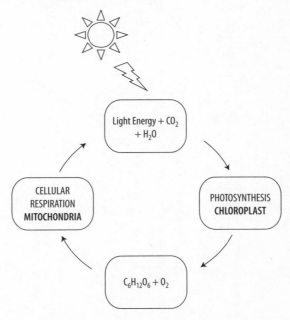

C. Electron transport and oxidative phosphorylation are examples of coupled reactions.

Fermentation and Cellular Respiration

I. Cellular Energetics—Fermentation and Cellular Respiration

A. Fermentation and Cellular Respiration

1. Both reactions are catabolic.
2. Chemical equation for cell respiration: $C_6H_{12}O_6 + 6O_2 \rightarrow 6CO_2 + 6H_2O + ATP$
3. Both involve *oxidation-reduction reactions*:
   i. Loss of electrons is oxidation (glucose to carbon dioxide).
   ii. Gain of electrons is reduction (oxygen to water).
   iii. *Electrons = Energy*
4. In cell respiration there are two "electron and hydrogen carrier molecules" that help carry the energy from glucose to the mitochondria where it will be harnessed—*NADH (Nicotinamide Adenine Dinucleotide)* and *FADH₂ (Flavin Adenine Dinucleotide)*.
   i. NAD^+ = oxidized form, NADH = reduced form
   ii. FAD = oxidized form, $FADH_2$ = reduced form

B. The Four Parts of Cellular Respiration

1. *Glycolysis—"splitting of sugar"*
   i. Takes place in the cytoplasm and is an anerobic process.
   ii. Oldest metabolic pathway since it is found in prokaryotes, which were the first organisms on earth.
   iii. The 6 carbon sugar, glucose, is broken down into two 3-carbon molecules called pyruvate. This is just a re-arrangement of the carbons from glucose.
   iv. Ten-step metabolic reaction that initially invests ATP that will yield a "small" energy payoff.

v. NAD^+ is reduced to NADH.

vi. End products of glycolysis are 2 pyruvate molecules, 2 NADH molecules, and 2 ATP via substrate level phosphorylation (2 of each molecule because of the splitting of the glucose molecule in step 4).

vii. *Substrate level phosphorylation*—formation of ATP via a direct transfer of phosphate from a donor molecule to ADP.

viii. There is no loss of CO_2 (decarboxylation) in glycolysis.

2. *Shuttle Step*—"*process of converting pyruvate to Acetyl CoA.*"

i. Takes place in the mitochondria.

ii. Pyruvate is decarboxylated to form acetate a 2-carbon compound. Acetate then has a coenzyme A group attached to it to form Acetyl Coenzyme A (Acetyl-CoA). NADH is made as a by-product via a reduction reaction.

$$\text{Pyrvuate (3 carbons)} \xrightarrow{\textit{yields}} \text{Acetyl-CoA (2 carbons)} + 2CO_2 + \text{NADH}$$

3. *Krebs Cycle*—"*generation of NADH and $FADH_2$.*"

i. Takes place in the mitochondrial matrix.

ii. Eight-step metabolic reaction that produces the majority of NADH, $FADH_2$, and CO_2 (waste product) for cellular respiration.

iii. Key intermediate to know: Oxaloacetate (OAA); the 2-carbon fragment from Acetyl Co-A is added to OAA to make citrate.

4. *Electron Transport Chain Coupled to Oxidative Phosphorylation*

i. The inner mitochondrial membrane or cristae is the site where Electron Transport Chain (ETC) proteins are found.

ii. Proteins in the ETC accept electrons from the electron carriers NADH and $FADH_2$. The cytochrome complex is a series of proteins in the ETC (evolutionary, conserved through time).

iii. Electrons get passed down the ETC via oxidation-reduction reactions until they meet the final electron acceptor molecule, oxygen (O_2), to form H_2O.

iv. In the ETC, no direct ATP is made; it must be coupled to Oxidative Phosphorylation via *chemiosmosis* (or the diffusion of H^+ ions across the membrane).

$$\text{Electron Transport Chain} \xrightarrow{\textit{Chemiosmosis}} \text{Oxidative Phosphorylation}$$

v. As NADH and $FADH_2$ are oxidized, H^+ inside the mitochondrial matrix is transported to the intermembrane space. A *proton motive force* (or storing of energy) is created across the membrane due to this transport. Once the H^+ is in the intermembrane space, it "leaks" back through the membrane by using an enzyme called *ATP synthase* and ATP is produced.

vi. Electrons that passed via NADH produce 3 ATP, while electrons from $FADH_2$ produce 2 ATP.

Cellular Respiration Scorecard

Step	Direct ATP from Substrate-Level Phosphorylation	NADH Produced	$FADH_2$ Produced
Glycolysis	2	2	0
Shuttle Step	0	2*	0
Krebs Cycle	2	6	2

*Could be $FADH_2$ depending on the type of shuttle: 1 NADH = 3 ATP; 1 $FAHD_2$ = 2 ATP

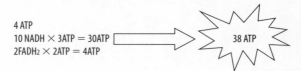

4 ATP
10 NADH $\times$ 3ATP = 30ATP
2FADH2 $\times$ 2ATP = 4ATP

38 ATP

C. Fermentation

1. *Lactic Acid Fermentation*—"*anaerobic process in which only glycolysis takes place.*"

   i. Takes place in prokaryotes and in humans.

   ii. Pyruvate is converted to lactic acid producing only 2 ATP and 2 NADH.

   iii. Prokaryotes can only use fermentation (glycolysis) because they have no mitochondria that are required for the other parts of cellular respiration.

   iv. In humans this anaerobic process (lack of oxygen to the muscles cells) causes the phenomenon of "the burn" in muscles cells. Vigorous exercise can cause lactic acid build-up and therefore cause muscle pain and fatigue.

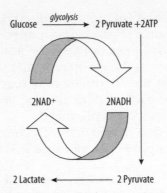

Glucose $\xrightarrow{\text{glycolysis}}$ 2 Pyruvate +2ATP

2NAD+   2NADH

2 Lactate ←——— 2 Pyruvate

2. *Alcoholic Fermentation—"anaerobic process in which only glycolysis takes place."*
   i.   Takes place in fungi, such as yeast, and is used in the beer and wine industry.
   ii. Pyruvate is converted to acetylaldehyde and then ethanol, producing only 2 ATP, 2NADH, and 2 CO_2.
   iii. Fungi have mitochondria, but in anaerobic conditions carry out this process.

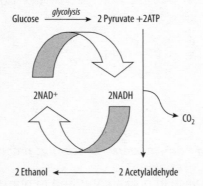

Glucose $\xrightarrow{\text{glycolysis}}$ 2 Pyruvate +2ATP

2NAD+   2NADH

CO_2

2 Ethanol ←——— 2 Acetylaldehyde

Molecules and Cells—*Don't stress out to learn the names of all the enzymes involved in cellular respiration. AP questions on this topic are designed for you to understand the "big picture" of cell respiration.*

Photosynthesis

I. Cellular Energetics—Photosynthesis

A. Autotrophs/Heterotrophs

1. Used by *autotrophs* or "self feeders"—organisms that create their own organic molecules or food. Autotrophs are also known as *producers*.
2. Plants are *photoautotrophs*—organisms that create their own organic molecules or food by using light energy.
3. *Heterotrophs*—organisms that cannot create their own organic molecules or food. Heterotrophs are *consumers*.
4. Photosynthesis takes place in the chloroplast of the plant.

B. The two parts of photosynthesis

1. *Light Dependent Reaction*—"process in which NADPH, ATP, and O_2 are produced."
   i. Accessory molecules to know in the light-dependent reaction:
      - *Chlorophyll a*—absorbs red light (680 nm) and purple light (400 nm).
      - *Chlorophyll b*—absorbs yellow light (650 nm) and blue light (450 nm).
      - *Carotenoids*—absorbs at various wavelengths and protects the chlorophyll molecules.
   ii. The accessory molecules absorb photons of light and become "excited" when their electrons gain energy.
   iii. *Photosystems*—light-gathering centers that contain chlorophyll and accessory molecules.
      - *Photosystem II*—P680—named such because light is absorbed best at 680 nm.

- *Photosystem I—P700—named such because light is absorbed best at 700 nm.*
iv. Route of electrons though *non-cyclic electron flow* of the light dependent reaction.

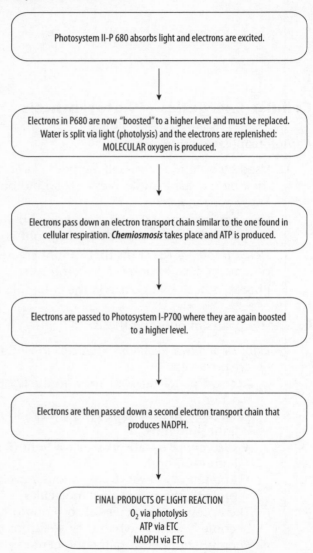

Photosystem II-P 680 absorbs light and electrons are excited.

Electrons in P680 are now "boosted" to a higher level and must be replaced. Water is split via light (photolysis) and the electrons are replenished: MOLECULAR oxygen is produced.

Electrons pass down an electron transport chain similar to the one found in cellular respiration. ***Chemiosmosis*** takes place and ATP is produced.

Electrons are passed to Photosystem I-P700 where they are again boosted to a higher level.

Electrons are then passed down a second electron transport chain that produces NADPH.

FINAL PRODUCTS OF LIGHT REACTION
O_2 via photolysis
ATP via ETC
NADPH via ETC

v. Route of electrons through *cyclic electron flow* of the light-dependent reaction.

- This reaction takes place by electrons cycling back from P700 through the first ETC. This has the net effect of producing ATP in greater amounts. No NADPH or O_2 is produced. This reaction takes place because the Calvin Cycle uses more ATP per mole than NADPH per mole, and hence replenishes the used ATP.

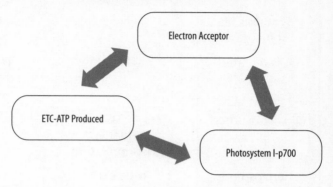

2. *Dark Reaction/Calvin Cycle/Light Independent Reaction— "process in which NADPH and ATP are used to make organic compounds such as glucose."*
   i. Uses the products of the light reaction (ATP and NADPH) to produce glucose.
   ii. Takes place in the stroma of the chloroplast.

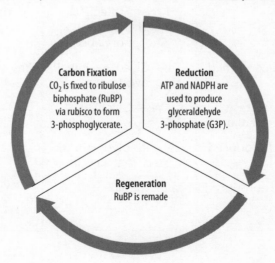

C. Comparison Chart

Process	Takes Place in Cellular Respiration	Takes Place in Photosynthesis
Breakdown of glucose	Yes	No
Synthesis of glucose	No	Yes—Calvin Cycle
O_2 is released	No	Yes—light-dependent reaction
O_2 is consumed	Yes—ETC and Oxidative Phosphorylation	No
Chemiosmosis	Yes—ETC	Yes—ETC
CO_2 is released	Yes—Shuttle Step and Krebs Cycle	No
CO_2 is consumed/ fixed	No	Yes—Calvin Cycle
ATP is produced	Yes—Glycolysis, Krebs Cycle, ETC and Oxidative Phosphorylation	Yes—light-dependent reaction
ATP is consumed	Yes—Glycolysis initial investment	Yes—Calvin Cycle
Pyruvate as intermediate	Yes—Glycolysis	No
NADH produced	Yes—Glycolysis, shuttle step, Krebs cycle	No
NADPH produced	No	Yes—light-dependent reaction

D. Alternatives to Photosynthesis

1. *Photorespiration*
   i. C_3 plants make up roughly 90% of the plants on earth and fix carbon into a 3-phosphoglycerate (3 carbon compound).
   ii. Normal photosynthetic processes take place within C_3 plants.
   iii. When the day is hot and/or dry, stomata are closed; therefore, less carbon dioxide enters the cell for the Dark Reaction. *Rubisco* will fix oxygen rather than carbon dioxide through a process called *photorespiration*. Photorespiration will produce no ATP and the Dark Reaction will not fix carbon, thus decreasing glucose output.

2. C_4 *Plants*
   i. Plants that prefer an alternative mode of carbon fixation that forms a four-carbon compound first rather than a three-carbon compound.
   ii. Leaf anatomy is the main reason why C_4 plants have alternative carbon fixation.
   iii. Bundle-sheath cells are found around the vein of the leaf, and the mesophyll cells are found between the bundle-sheath cells and the leaf surface.

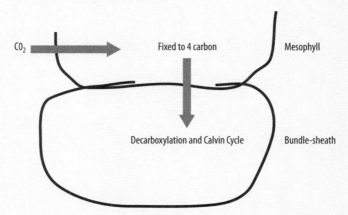

CO_2 Fixed to 4 carbon   Mesophyll

Decarboxylation and Calvin Cycle   Bundle-sheath

iv. C$_4$ plants minimize photorespiration because the enzyme Rubisco is not as available to fix oxygen. A secondary enzyme called PEP carboxylase fixes the carbon dioxide to a four-carbon compound and has no affinity for oxygen. C$_4$ plants fix carbon dioxide more efficiently than C$_3$ plants.

3. *Crassulacean Acid Metabolism (CAM) Plants*
   i. Based on arid conditions and plants that are succulent (water-storing).
   ii. At night, CAM plants open their stomata and during the day close their stomata.
   iii. Closing the stomata during the day halts the drying out of the plant, but also prevents carbon dioxide from entering.
   iv. Opening the stomata during the night allows the plant to take in carbon dioxide where it will be stored in the form of organic acids.

Test Tip

***Molecules and Cells**—Some similarities between cellular respiration and photosynthesis are always tested on the AP Biology exam. Included are the following: ATP production, electron transport use, compartmentalization between chloroplast and mitochondria, hydrogen and electron acceptor molecules, such as NADH, FADH$_2$, and NADPH.*

PART III:

HEREDITY AND EVOLUTION: Heredity, Molecular Genetics, and Evolutionary Biology

Meiosis and Gametogenesis

I. Heredity—Meiosis and Gametogenesis

A. Genetic Terms

1. *Genes*—heredity units made up of DNA.
2. *Locus*—a gene's specific location on the chromosome.
3. *Asexual Reproduction*—a form of reproduction not requiring meiosis or fertilization. Only passes a copy of genes to its progeny. A type of reproduction in which there is no variation in genetic make-up. Bacteria reproduce via asexual reproduction.
4. *Clone*—an individual that arises from asexual reproduction.
5. *Sexual Reproduction*—a type of reproduction that involves variation because two parents give rise to their progeny. Major evolutionary advantage because of genetic variation.
6. *Somatic Cell*—a body cell that is diploid.
7. *Gamete*—a sex cell such as egg or sperm.

Life Cycles of Animals and Plants

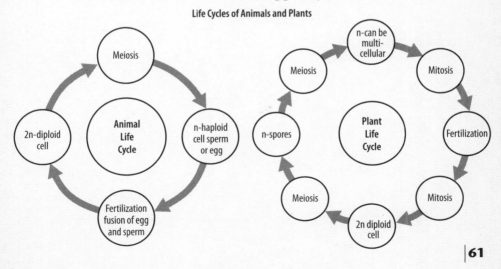

B. Meiosis—Key Points

1. Meiosis, like mitosis, is preceded by replication of chromosomes.

2. Unlike mitosis, meiosis has two consecutive cell divisions called Meiosis I and II.

3. Division results in four daughter cells that are genetically different and are haploid.

4. Tetrads are formed or the pairing of homologous chromosomes via *synapsis*. *Chiasmata* or the site of crossing over/exchange of genetic material is formed in Prophase I of Meiosis I.

5. In Metaphase I of Meiosis I homologous chromosomes pair with each other at the metaphase plate.

6. Homologous chromosomes separate in Anaphase I of Meiosis I and sister chromatids stay together.

7. Meiosis II has no further chromosomal replications and looks just like Mitosis.

8. Chromosomes will independently assort from each other producing variations.

9. Crossing over in Prophase I is another mechanism for variation from meiosis.

C. Comparison of Mitosis and Meiosis

Event	Mitosis	Meiosis
DNA Replication	Occurs during interphase	Occurs during interphase
Homologous Chromosomes	Align one after another on metaphase plate	Pair with each other during metaphase I. Align one after another on metaphase plate during metaphase II
Sister Chromatid Separation	Anaphase	Meiosis II Anaphase II
Divisions	1	2
Cells Produced	2 Diploid—genetically identical	4 Haploid—genetically different
Crossing Over	Does not occur	Meiosis I Prophase I

Test Tip

Molecules and Cells—*Every AP Biology test-taker should know the main differences between meiosis and mitosis. Mitosis produces diploid identical cells that have no genetic variation. Meiosis produces gametes (haploid) that are genetically different because of crossing over in Prophase I of meiosis. Similarly, know the stages of mitosis and meiosis and special structures that are formed.*

Eukaryotic Chromosomes

I. ## Heredity—Eukaryotic Chromosomes

A. Structure and Function of Eukaryotic Chromosome

Part	Structure	Function
Genes	Made up of the nucleic acid DNA	Will be transcribed onto mRNA Will be translated for proteins
Chromatids	Two replicated chromosomes that are held together at the centromere	Allows proper segregation of chromosome during meiosis and mitosis
Centromere	DNA region found near the middle (not always) chromosome	Hold chromatids together to form a chromosome.
Chromatin	DNA and protein combination	Aids in packaging DNA, DNA replication, and expression of proteins
Kinetochore	Proteins	Allows for the attachment of the mitotic spindle to the centromere
Nucleosomes	Histone proteins and DNA	Aids in packaging of DNA
Telomeres	Ends of DNA	Protection against the destruction of the DNA from nucleases
Remember: Eukaryotic DNA is linear, meaning it has definite ends. Most eukaryotic organisms are diploid. Fungi, such as yeast, can exist as haploid or diploid.		

B. Advantages to Chromosomes

1. Genetic variation—crossing over, independent assortment.
2. Gene regulation
3. Allows for a large number of genes to be expressed.
4. Diploid—allows one to have two copies of genes as a backup mechanism.
5. Linkage of genes to be inherited together.

C. Structure and Function of Prokaryotic Chromosome as a Comparison

1. Circular in shape and much smaller than eukaryotic chromosome.
2. Genes are arranged in *operons*—one promoter controlling many genes.
3. Transcription and translation are coupled processes.
4. *Plasmids* are prevalent—extra chromosomal pieces of DNA that carry antibiotic resistance. They are not part of the chromosome. Autonomously replicating.
5. One origin of replication.
6. No histone proteins to condense, but DNA is supercoiled.

Inheritance Patterns

I. Heredity—Inheritance Patterns

A. Inheritance Terms

1. *Characteristic*—a heritable feature such as hair color (phenotype).
2. *Trait*—a variant of a characteristic. Example: red or blond hair color.
3. *Allele*—alternative form of a gene, such as tall (*T*) plants are dominant to short plants (*t*).
4. *Dominant allele*—the allele that is fully expressed.
5. *Recessive allele*—the allele that is not expressed.
6. *Genotype*—the genetic makeup of an organism.
7. *Phenotype*—organism's appearance.
8. *Gregor Mendel*—father of genetics who worked on genetic crosses of pea plants.
9. *Law of Segregation*—separation of alleles into gametes.

B. Genetic Crosses

1. *Monohybrid cross*—a cross that tracks the inheritance pattern of a single character.
   Example: In pea plants, tall (*T*) plants are dominant to short plants (*t*). There are three allelic combinations:
   ➤ *TT*—homozygous dominant (considered true breeding)/Tall
   ➤ *Tt*—heterozygous or hybrid/Tall
   ➤ *tt*—homozygous recessive (considered true breeding)/Short

Cross two true breeding plants of tall and short

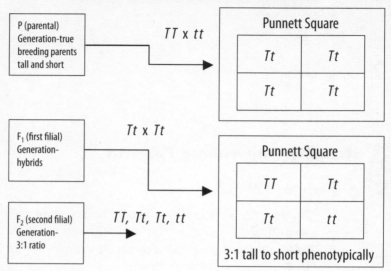

P (parental) Generation-true breeding parents tall and short	*TT* x *tt*	Punnett Square	
		Tt	*Tt*
		Tt	*Tt*

F₁ (first filial) Generation-hybrids	*Tt* x *Tt*	Punnett Square	
		TT	*Tt*
F₂ (second filial) Generation-3:1 ratio	*TT, Tt, Tt, tt*	*Tt*	*tt*
		3:1 tall to short phenotypically	

2. *Test cross*—A cross that determines whether the dominant parent is homozygous dominant or heterozygous. Always cross the dominant parent to a homozygous recessive. Assume black (B) is dominant to white (b) for cat coat color.

Black parent could be BB or Bb. White parent is bb.
➤ If BB x bb, all progeny will be black carriers.

➤ If Bb x bb, ½ of the progeny are black and ½ are white.

3. *Law of Independent Assortment*—is observed with dihybrid crosses or crosses between two different characters. Alleles assort independently from each other; therefore, dominant can combine with recessive.

Example: In pea plants, tall (*T*) plants are dominant to short plants (*t*). Green leaf (*G*) is dominant to yellow leaf (g).

Cross two true breeding plants of tall green and short yellow

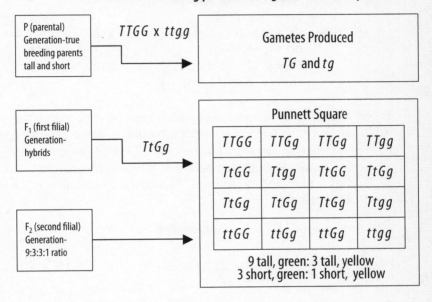

P (parental) Generation-true breeding parents tall and short	*TTGG* x *ttgg*	Gametes Produced *TG* and *tg*			

F₁ (first filial) Generation-hybrids	*TtGg*	Punnett Square			
		TTGG	*TTGg*	*TTGg*	*TTgg*
		TtGG	*Ttgg*	*TtGG*	*TtGg*
F₂ (second filial) Generation-9:3:3:1 ratio		*TtGg*	*TtGg*	*TtGg*	*Ttgg*
		ttGG	*ttGg*	*ttGg*	*ttgg*

9 tall, green: 3 tall, yellow:
3 short, green: 1 short, yellow

C. Using the Laws of Probability in Genetics

1. *The law of multiplication*—independent events are governed by this; therefore, for genes that are linked the law of multiplication cannot be followed.

   i. Assume the following cross: AaBbCc x AabbCC. What are the chances of the following progeny?
      a) AabbCC
      b) aabbCc
      c) AAbbCC

   Answer: Perform each individual monohybrid cross and use the law of multiplication.

   Aa x Aa = 1/2 Aa, 1/4 aa, 1/4 AA
   Bb x bb = 1/2 Bb, 1/2 bb
   Cc x CC = 1/2 Cc, 1/2 CC

a) AabbCC = 1/2 x 1/2 x 1/2 = 1/8
b) aabbCc = 1/4 x 1/2 x 1/2 = 1/16
c) AAbbCC = 1/4 x 1/2 x 1/2 = 1/16

ii. Assume the following genotype: *AaBBCcddEeFf*. How many different gametes are possible?

Answer: Determine how many different gametes are possible for each set of alleles.

Aa = 2 (either A or a) ⎤
BB = 1 (only B)   ⎥
Cc = 2 (either C or c) ⎥ 2 x 1 x 2 x 1 x 2 x 2 =
dd = 1 (only d)   ⎥ 16 different gametes
Ee = 2 (either E or e) ⎥
Ff = 2 (either F or f) ⎦

D. Non-Mendelian Genetics—genetics that do not follow the inheritance patterns of Mendel's initial pea plant experiments.

1. *Incomplete dominance*—the phenotype of the offspring has an appearance that is between that of both parents. This is not a blending hypothesis. The dominant allele is not fully expressed.

Snapdragons

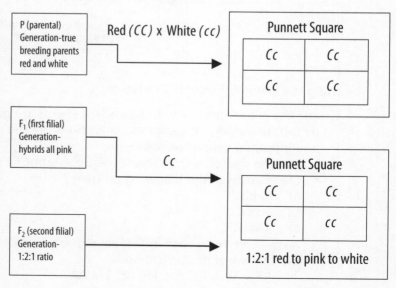

2. *Codominance*—both alleles are expressed at the same time.
   ➤ MN Blood system (M and N are blood group antigens found on the cell surface of a red blood cell).
   ➤ There are three allelic combinations:
     • *MM*—homozygous dominant (only produce M antigen on cell surface).
     • *MN*—heterozygous (produce M and N antigens on cell surface).
     • *NN*—homozygous recessive (only produce N antigen on cell surface).
3. *Multiple Alleles*—many different alleles can control the expression of a character.
   i. ABO Blood System—carbohydrate antigens found on the cell surface.

Geno-type	Phenotype	Antigen on Cell Surface of Red Blood Cell	Antibodies Present in Blood
ii	O blood type	None	Anti A, Anti B
$I^A I^A$ or $I^A i$	A blood type	B	Anti A
$I^B I^B$ or $I^B i$	B blood type	A	Anti B
$I^A I^B$	AB blood type	AB	None

Example ABO Cross: Assume that a child has type B blood and the father was type A. What are the possible genotypes of the mother?

Answer: Child could be $I^B I^B$ or $I^B i$ and the father had to be $I^A i$. The mother could be either $I^B I^B$ or $I^B i$ or $I^A I^B$. If the father was $I^A I^A$ no matter what genotype the mother is, a type B child could not be produced.

4. *Pleiotropy*—one gene causes multiple different phenotypic effects on an organism.

Human Disease PKU (phenylketouria) Phenotypes		
Mental Retardation	Hair Loss	Skin Pigmentation

5. *Epistasis*—one gene affecting the expression of another gene. F_2 offspring phenotypic ratio is usually 9:3:4.

6. *Polygenic inheritance*—two or more genes affecting one phenotype. Examples include skin color and cancer, which is the most common polygenic inherited disorder. Polygenic inheritance leads to a bell curve distribution of phenotypes.

E. *Pedigree Analysis*—a visual depiction of inheritance patterns in multiple family generations.

1. Basic Rules
   i. If two affected people have an unaffected child, it must be a dominant pedigree: [A] is the dominant mutant allele and [a] is the recessive allele. Both parents are Aa (hybrid carriers) and the unaffected child is aa.
   ii. If two unaffected people have an affected child, it is a recessive pedigree: [A] is the dominant allele and [a] is the recessive allele. Both parents are Aa (hybrid carriers) and the affected child is aa.
   iii. If every affected person has an affected parent, it is a dominant pedigree (no skipping of generations).
   iv. Dominant traits never skip generations, while recessive traits can skip.
   v. Squares are male.
   vi. Circles are females.
   vii. Mating is indicated by the connection with a line.

   viii. Filled-in circles or squares indicate affected person.

   ix. Sex-linked dominant—all females descending from the affected males have the disease.
   x. Sex-linked recessive—no male carriers possible and skips generations.
   xi. Autosomal recessive—carriers are present, so skips generations. 50% males and females affected.

xii. Autosomal dominant—no carriers or skipping of generations. 50% males and females affected.

F. Autosomal Genetic Disorders

Recessive Inherited Disorder—absence or malfunction of protein Must receive both non-functional copies from parents; therefore, affected individual is homozygous recessive (aa).	
Disease	**Outcome**
Albinism	Lack of pigment in the skin, eyes, and hair. May lead to skin cancers.
Cystic Fibrosis	Defective or absent chloride channel protein in membranes, causing a build-up of mucus in lungs. Person is prone to bacterial infections.
Tay-Sachs	Defective or absent lipase enzyme in brain. Predominant in Jewish population.
Sickle cell disease	Defective hemoglobin protein. Mostly affects the African-American population.

Dominant Inherited Disorder—absence or malfunction of protein Must receive at least one non-functional copy from one parent; therefore, affected individual is heterozygous (Aa) or homozygous dominant (AA).	
Disease	**Outcome**
Achondroplasia	Dwarfism
Huntington's Disease	Degenerative breakdown of the nervous system.

G. Linked Genes

1. Thomas Hunt Morgan performed genetic crosses with the fruit fly *(Drosophila melanogaster)*

2. Terms used in fruit fly crosses.
    i. *Wild Type*—most common phenotype in the population.
    ii. *Mutants*—alternative phenotypes to the wild type.
3. Morgan performed the following dihybrid mating:
    ➤ Example: In fruit flies, gray (g^+) body color is dominant to black body color (g). Normal wings (w^+) are dominant to dumpy wings (w).
    ➤ Cross a double heterozygote to a double recessive (g^+g w^+w x ggww).
    ➤ Expected phenotypes of 1000 offspring would be:
    250 wild type (gray normal)/parental phenotype
    250 black dumpy/parental phenotype
    250 gray dumpy/recombinant phenotype
    250 black normal/recombinant phenotype
    ➤ Observed phenotypes of 1000 offspring were:
    450 wild type (gray normal) /parental phenotype
    450 black dumpy/parental phenotype
    50 gray dumpy/recombinant phenotype
    50 black normal/recombinant phenotype

The high number of observed parental phenotypes indicated that the genes for body color and wings were linked to each other. Linked genes are on the same chromosome and are very close to each other. Linked genes are inherited together and recombination between the genes is very low.

    ➤ Calculation of Recombination Frequency or the measure of genetic linkage between 2 genes (also called map units).

$$\text{Recombination Frequency} = \frac{\text{\# of recombinants}}{\text{total offspring}} \times 100$$

Using the data above:

$$\text{Recombination Frequency} = \frac{100}{1000} \times 100 = 10\%$$

Only 10% of the time will there be recombination between the genes for body type and wings.

4. Genetic Maps
    i. Recombination Frequency allows you to create genetic maps that estimate the distance between genes.

    ii. Assume the following Recombination Frequencies. Determine the genetic map for genes W,X,Y, Z
        W-Y, 7 map units
        W-X, 26 map units
        W-Z, 24 map units
        Y-X, 19 map units
        Y-Z, 31 map units

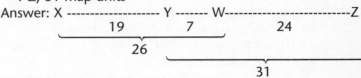

Answer: X -------------------- Y ------- W--------------------------Z
                  19   7   24
                       26
                              31

5. Sex-linked genes
   i. Genes that are carried on the X-chromosome.
   ii. Females carry two X chromosomes, XX.
   iii. Males carry 1X and 1Y, XY.
   iv. Inheritance patterns of sex-linked genes:
      1. A father will always transmit the sex-linked trait to his daughter. His son receives the Y, and does not inherit the trait.
      2. Only females can be carriers of sex-linked traits. Therefore, a carrier female who mates with a normal male transmits the mutant allele to half her sons and half her daughters.
      3. Examples of sex-linked traits include hemophilia and muscular dystrophy.
   v. *Barr body*—one of the female's X chromosomes is randomly inactivated in order to have the same gene dosage as males for sex chromosomes. The chromosome tends to look smaller in physical structure. Example of the phenotypic output of X-inactivation are Calico-colored cats.

6. Chromosomal Mutations
   i. Non-disjunction of chromosomes
      1. If non-disjunction takes place in Meiosis I, all 4 cells will be *aneuploid*, or have abnormal chromosome numbers. 2 cells will be *monosomic* (n-1) and 2 cells will be *trisomic* (n+1).
      2. If non-disjunction takes place in Meiosis II, 2 cells will be normal (n), 1 cell (n-1) monosomic, and 1 cell trisomic (n+1).

ii. *Polyploidy*—having more than two chromosome sets such as triploid (3N).

iii. *Deletion*—entire fragment of chromosome is lost.

iv. *Duplication*—entire fragment of chromosome is duplicated on the chromosome.

v. *Inversion*—part of the chromosome reverses its orientation.

vi. *Translocation*—one part of a chromosome is attached to another part of a different chromosome.

vii. *Down Syndrome or Trisomy 21*—presence of all or part of an extra chromosome 21.

viii. *XXY*—Klinefelter syndrome. Phenotypically male, but are sterile and have reduced testes size and enlarged breasts.

ix. *XO*—Turner syndrome. Phenotypically female, but have a lack of development of secondary female characteristics.

x. *Fragile X*—abnormal X chromosome, which causes mental retardation and autism.

Test Tip

Heredity and Evolution—*You may have to perform simple Mendelian crosses that are either monohydrid or dihydrid. This may require you to work backwards from data to find the genotypes of parents.*

RNA and DNA Structure and Function

I. Molecular Genetics—RNA and DNA Structure and Function

A. Deoxyribonucleic Acid (DNA)—Genetic material

B. Ribonucleic Acid (RNA)

1. 3 types: mRNA (messenger RNA), rRNA (ribosomal RNA), tRNA (transfer RNA)
2. All 3 are involved in the expression of genes into proteins.

C. Nucleotides

1. Nucleic acids are made of nucleotides. A nucleotide is composed of a 5 carbon sugar, a nitrogenous base, and a phosphate group.
2. Two types of nitrogenous bases: purines (6-member ring fused to a 5-member ring) and pyrimidines (6-member ring).

Purines	Pyrimidines
Adenine	Thymine (not found in RNA)
Guanine	Cytosine
	Uracil (only found in RNA)

3. Two types of sugars: deoxyribose for DNA and ribose for RNA.
4. Phosphate group (see chapter on Molecules and Cells).
5. Nucleoside is a nitrogenous base and sugar without the phosphate.

Discovery of DNA as the Genetic Material

A. Transformation Experiments of Griffith, Avery, McCarty, MacLeod.

1. Smooth (contains capsule) living *Streptococcus pneumonia* injected into live mouse, resulted in a dead mouse.
2. Rough (no capsule) living *Streptococcus pneumonia* injected into live mouse, resulted in a healthy mouse.
3. Heat-killed smooth (capsule destroyed) *Streptococcus pneumonia* injected into live mouse, resulted in a healthy mouse.
4. Heat-killed smooth (contains capsule) mixed with living rough (no capsule) *Streptococcus pneumonia* injected into live mouse, resulted in a dead mouse.
5. Interpretation of the experiment was that the DNA from the heat-killed smooth cells "transformed" the rough cells into smooth cells that killed the mouse. Transforming agent was DNA.

B. Hershey-Chase Experiment

1. Worked with T2 bacteriophage or a virus that infects bacteria.
2. Bacteriophage were radioactively labeled with P32 (DNA) or S35 (protein coat of bacteriophage).
3. When separate experiments were completed, it was found that bacteria contain the radioactively labeled P32 DNA of the bacteriophage.
4. Interpretation of the experiment was that the bacteriophage injected their DNA into the host bacterium in order to produce progeny phage, indicating DNA as the genetic material.

C. Watson and Crick

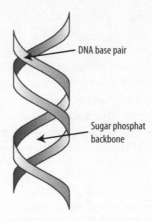

DNA base pair

Sugar phosphat backbone

1. James Watson and Francis Crick used X-ray crystallography experiments to show that DNA is a double helix.
2. Data of the experiment also indicated that the double helix had a sugar phosphate backbone with nitrogenous bases pairing interior to the double helix.
3. Base pairing rules of purines and pyrimidines were established (also known as Chargaff's rule).
    i. Adenine (purine) pairs with thymine (pyrimidine). 2 hydrogen bonds for base pairing.
    ii. Guanine (purine) pairs with cytosine (pyrimidine). 3 hydrogen bonds for base pairing.

Hydrogen bonds indicated by dashed lines.

Adenine   Thymine

Guanine   Cytosine

D. Meselson-Stahl

1. Experiment indicated that replication of DNA is semi-conservative, or one old strand is used for the synthesis (template) of a new strand.

2. Experiment showed that both heavy and light nitrogen would be incorporated into the daughter DNA during the first round of DNA replication. In the second round of replication, daughter strands would only have light nitrogen since the heavy nitrogen was removed. Banding patterns indicated a semi-conservative model is favored over conservative or dispersive.

Heredity and Evolution—*Every AP Biology test-taker should know the main differences between DNA and RNA. DNA consists of A, T, C, G as nitrogenous bases, deoxyribose as 5 carbon sugar, and phosphate. RNA consists of A, U, G, C as nitrogenous bases, ribose as 5 carbon sugar, and phosphate. Structurally DNA is a double-stranded helix, while RNA is single-stranded.*

III. DNA Replication

1. Where does DNA replication begin?
   i. Origins of replication (Ori) or specific DNA sequences where replication will commence. In prokaryotes there is one origin for replication while in eukaryotes there are thousands of origins for replication.
   ii. DNA replication proceeds in both directions on the strand, forming what is called a replication fork.

2. Elongation
   i. Elongation at the replication fork is catalyzed by an enzyme called DNA polymerase.

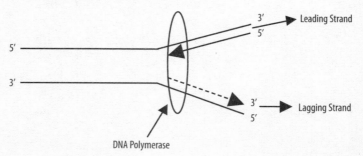

ii. Nucleotides are the substrate for DNA polymerase and ATP is hydrolyzed by the enzyme.

iii. Strands have to be primed by an enzyme called RNA primase. This enzyme adds a small strand of RNA for DNA polymerase to hook to and begin the synthesis of a new DNA strand. The RNA primer is removed later in replication and filled in with DNA.

iv. The two strands of DNA are anti-parallel or 5' phosphate to 3' hydroxyl in one direction and at the opposite end is 3' hydroxyl to 5' phosphate.

v. DNA polymerase only elongates the strand from 5' to 3'.

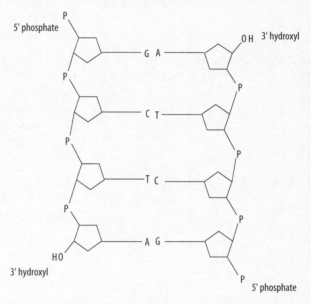

vi. Leading Strand—the daughter strand that is synthesized into the replication fork. This strand is synthesized in a continuous fashion.

vii. Lagging Strand—the daughter strand that is synthesized away from the replication fork. This strand is synthesized in a discontinuous fashion or in fragments called Okazaki fragments.

viii. DNA ligase is the enzyme that will take a 5' phosphate and 3' hydroxyl and link them together, helping join the Okazaki fragments into a single strand.

Major Enzymes and Proteins in DNA Replication		
Enzyme	**Substrate**	**Action**
DNA helicase	Double-stranded DNA	Opens up the DNA strand for replication
Single-stranded binding proteins	Single-stranded DNA	Binds single-stranded DNA and keeps replication fork open
DNA primase	Single-stranded DNA	Lays down a RNA primer on single-stranded DNA for DNA polymerase to hook up with
DNA polymerase	Single-stranded DNA	Adds the complementary base to the daughter strand using the parental template. Follows base pairing rules; adenine with thymine, guanine with cytosine
DNA ligase	Single-stranded DNA	Links a 5' phosphate with a 3' hydroxyl on the lagging strand

Gene Regulation

I. Molecular Genetics—Gene Regulation

A. One Gene-One Enzyme Hypothesis of Beadle and Tatum

   1. Used *auxotrophs* (nutritional mutants) of *Neurospora crassa.*
   2. Wild type can grow on a minimal media while several other class mutants were not able to grow on minimal media unless supplemented.
   3. Each mutant had a specific metabolic deficiency because the gene that produced the required enzyme was mutated.

B. Transcription

   1. Synthesis of single-stranded mRNA (messenger RNA) from DNA.
   2. Nuclear event.
   3. Major enzyme involved is RNA polymerase, and runs in a 5' to 3' direction.
   4. RNA polymerase binds to a promoter or sequence in the DNA that allows for the initiation of transcription. Part of the promoter has a sequence of 5'TATAAA3' called TATA box.
   5. Eukaryotic cell transcription factors along with RNA polymerase promote transcription.
   6. Complementary base pair in RNA is different from that found in DNA. The base pairing is adenine with uracil and guanine with cytosine.
   7. Termination of transcription requires a sequence in the DNA called the *terminator.*

8. mRNA in eukaryotes is modified after it is synthesized from RNA polymerase. A poly A tail and 5' 7-methylguanosine cap are added to aid in the stability of the message.

9. RNA splicing is a process in which nonprotein coding portions of pre-mRNA called *introns* are excised, while coding portions called *exons* are spliced together to form a fully functional mRNA molecule. Protein complex called the *spliceosome* catalyzes this cut-and-paste mechanism.

C. Translation

1. Synthesis of protein from mRNA in the 5' to 3' direction.

2. Takes place in the cytoplasm and the rough ER.

3. Requires all 3 RNA molecules (mRNA, tRNA, and rRNA) and codons (sets of 3 nucleotide RNA bases that code for amino acids).

4. As mRNA threads itself through the ribosome, initiation of the process begins with a location of the start codon AUG (calls for the amino acid methionine).

5. Once the start codon is found, a t-RNA molecule containing the appropriate amino acid is brought to the ribosome. The tRNA molecule binds to the codon via an anticodon complementary sequence which is located on tRNA. Once the binding happens, the entire ribosome translocates down another 3 bases and reads another codon sequence, where another tRNA brings in the appropriate amino acid. A peptide bond between amino acids is formed via an enzymatic reaction promoted by the rRNA portion of the ribosome.

6. Termination of translation happens when one of the following codons is read: UAA, UGA, UAG.

Mutation

I. Molecular Genetics—Mutation

A. Mutation—changes in the genetic material.

1. Two types of point mutations: Base pair substitution and base pair insertions or deletions.

2. Mutagens—Physical or chemical agents that promote mutations. Examples include UV light, X-rays, and chemicals such as bromine or chlorine.

Name of Mutation	Example	Consequence
Base Pair Substitution Silent Mutation	Wild Type mRNA AUG-CCU-UAC Protein MET-PRO-TYR Mutant mRNA AUG-CCG-UAC Protein MET-PRO-TYR	No change in protein sequence because the genetic code is redundant.
Base Pair Substitution Missense Mutation	Wild Type mRNA AUG-CCU-UAC Protein MET-PRO-TYR Mutant mRNA AUG-CCU-UGC Protein MET-PRO-CYS	Change in protein sequence because the UGC calls for a different amino acid. Most likely will change the structure, thus the function of protein.

(continued)

Name of Mutation	Example	Consequence

Base Pair Substitution Nonsense Mutation	Wild Type mRNA
	    AUG-CCU-UAC
	Protein MET-PRO-TYR
	Mutant mRNA
	    AUG-CCU-UAA
	Protein MET-PRO-STOP
		Premature stop codon put into protein. Protein is usually nonfunctional.

Insertion or Deletion Single Base Pair	Wild Type mRNA
	    AUG-CCU-UAC
	Protein MET-PRO-TYR
	Mutant mRNA
	    AUG-CCA-UUA-C
	Protein MET-PRO-LEU
		Change in protein sequence because of the shifting of the sequence by the addition of a base. Similarly can happen if one base is deleted. Protein is usually nonfunctional.

Insertion or Deletion Three Base Pair	Wild Type mRNA
	    AUG-CCU-UAC
	Protein MET-PRO-TYR
	Mutant mRNA
	    AUG-CCU-UAC-UUU
	Protein MET-PRO-TYR-
	    PHE
		Addition or loss of amino acid due to insertion or deletion of 3 bases. Protein will most likely retain some normal function.

Viral Structure and Replication, Bacterial Gene Regulation

I. **Viral Structure and Replication, Bacterial Gene Regulation**

A. Genome

1. Various types of genomes including the following: double-stranded DNA, single-stranded DNA, double-stranded RNA, or single-stranded RNA.

B. Capsids and Envelopes

1. Protein coat that protects the viral genome is called a *capsid*.
2. *Viral envelopes*—extra protection layer that surrounds the capsid.

C. Viral Reproduction

1. *Host cells*—the virus will invade and eventually live off of the host by taking over the metabolic machinery (parasitic). Viruses cannot reproduce independently.
2. *Interferon*—class of drugs produced by cells in response to viral infection.
3. Virus attaches to the host via cell surface receptors and injects its DNA.
4. *Lytic Cycle*—type of viral reproduction that eventually kills the host.
5. *Lysogenic Cycle*—virus will replicate its genome, but does not kill the host. Formation of *prophage*, or incorporation of the viral DNA into the host chromosome.

D. Human Immunodeficiency Virus or HIV, the causative agent of Acquired Immune Deficiency Syndrome (AIDS)

1. *Retrovirus*—RNA virus that uses an enzyme called *reverse transcriptase* to synthesize DNA from an RNA strand.
2. Infects T4 helper cells.

E. *Prion*—protein infectious particle or misfolded protein that converts other normal proteins into a mutant form. Causative agent for "mad cow disease."

II. Bacterial Gene Regulation

A. *Plasmid*—autonomous piece of self-replicating DNA.

B. Genetic Recombination in Bacteria

1. *Transformation*—bacteria uptaking DNA from an outside source. This is the crux of the Griffith, Avery, McCarty, MacLeod experiment outlined in Chapter 16.
2. *Transduction*—bacteriophages acting as vectors by moving bacterial genes from one bacterial cell and transferring to another.
3. *Conjugation*—formation of sex pilus between two bacteria that allows them to share genes with each other.
4. *Transposons*—transposable genetic elements or jumping genes. Genes being moved from one location to another in the cell's genome.

C. The Lactose Operon

1. *Operon*—sets of genes under the control of promoter.
2. *Lactose Operon*—operon required for the utilization of lactose as a carbon source.
   i. *Structural genes*—lacZ, lacY, lacA
   ii. *Regulatory genes*—lacI (repressor)
3. All bacterial gene regulation is done through the interaction of repressor proteins with specific DNA sequences called operators (found in the promoter region of a gene).

4. Repressor proteins bind to the operator sequence, acting as a blockade to stop RNA polymerase from binding to the promoter.

5. When the inducer is present, it will bind to the repressor, causing it to fall off the operator allowing RNA polymerase to transcribe the structural genes of the pathway.

6. The interplay of the inducer and repressor is the "hallmark" of bacterial gene regulation.

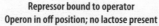

Repressor bound to operator
Operon in off position; no lactose present

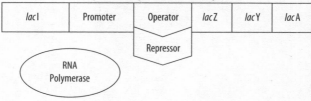

Repressor not bound to operator
Operon in on position; lactose present

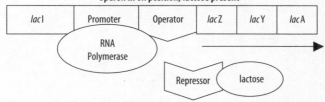

Gene	Product	Action
*lac*I	Repressor	Shuts operon off
*lac*Z	Beta-galactosidase	Breaks down lactose
*lac*Y	Permease	Allows lactose in cell
*lac*A	Transacetylase	Modifies lactose breakdown

Test Tip

***Heredity and Evolution**—The classic example of gene expression is the Lactose Operon. It is a good example to compare and contrast with eukaryotic gene expression in essays.*

Nucleic Acid Technology and Applications

I. DNA Cloning

1. *Restriction Enzymes*—enyzmes that cut DNA at particular sequences called restriction sites.

   Example: *Restriction site*

   ```
   -----ACTGGA----              -----A    CTGGA----
   -----TGACCT----    ------>    -----TGACC    T----
   ```

2. *Recombinant DNA*—combining DNA sequences that would not normally occur together to form one piece of DNA. The enzyme DNA ligase is added to seal the strands together.

   | -----A CTGGA---- + | | -----A ____ CTGGA---- |

   Cut DNA *Foreign DNA* *DNA Ligase* *Recombinant DNA*

3. *Cloning Vector*—original plasmid that is used to carry foreign DNA into a cell and replicate there.

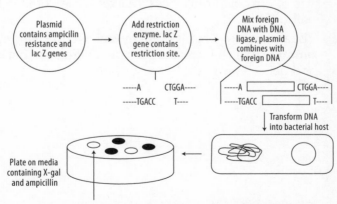

   Bacterial clone that is white and grows on plate is clone containing recombinant DNA plasmid.

   (See explanation on next page.)

1. When the restriction enzyme is added to plasmid, *lac Z* is destroyed and non-functional. The *lac Z* gene produces the enzyme β-galactosidase, which breaks down the sugar X-gal causing the colony to appear blue. If the *lac Z* gene product is not made, the colony appears white; if the gene is functional the colony appears blue.
2. Ampicillin resistance gene allows bacteria to grow in the presence of the antibiotic ampicillin.
3. Media is selective for clones that have the ampicillin resistance gene, and differential for blue or white colonies.
4. Colony that is growing on plate (ampicillin resistance) and white are correct clones carrying recombinant DNA.

II. DNA Gel Electrophoresis

1. DNA is placed in gel made of a polysaccharide called agarose or acrylamide (used for smaller fragments).
2. Migration of DNA is based on size differential of DNA fragments. An electric field is passed through DNA molecules and the molecules will travel toward the positive end (cathode) due to negative charge of phosphate on DNA.
3. Larger molecules travel slower, smaller molecules travel faster.
4. Marker DNA of a standard size is used to approximate the size of unknown molecules. Marker is measured in kilobase pairs.
5. Visualization of DNA is done by staining gel with ethidium bromide, which increases the visual difference between DNA and gel.

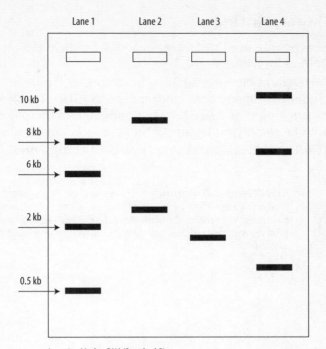

Lane 1 – Marker DNA/Standard Size
Lane 2 – 2 bands roughly 9 kb and 3 kb
Lane 3 – 1 band roughly 1.8 kb
Lane 4 – 3 bands roughly 12 kb, 7 kb, and 1 kb

Electrophoresis can be used for DNA and protein identification, isolation of types of DNA or protein, calculating the size of fragments (DNA and protein), crime scene investigation, and genetic testing.

III. Polymerase Chain Reaction

1. A method to take a small amount of DNA and amplify the amount.
2. Based on progressive heating and cooling of DNA strands with the addition of primers and DNA polymerase.

IV. DNA Fingerprinting

1. A technique used by forensic scientists to help determine the DNA of individuals.

2. The DNA of humans is highly homologous. There are sequences called *Short Tandem Repeats* (STR). These repeats vary in length and size for each human, and therefore, can be used as identifying factors of humans.

3. STRs can be visualized using DNA gel electrophoresis.

Heredity and Evolution—*Fully understanding the cloning process is considered a major concept in the AP Biology curriculum. You should understand how restriction enzymes and vectors are used in tandem to construct a recombinant plasmid.*

Early Evolution of Life

I. Early Evolution of Life

A. Earth and Early Life

1. Earth is most likely around 5 billion years old.

2. *Anaerobic prokaryotes* emerged approximately 4 billion years ago and represent the first origin of life.

3. Earliest living organisms were unicellular, had a genetic code, and were able to evolve and reproduce.

4. Prokaryotes diverged into two types—bacteria and archaea—about 2.5 billion years ago.

5. Oxygen accumulated in the atmosphere approximately 2.5 million years ago as a result of photosynthetic bacteria.

6. Eukaryotes emerged 2 billion years ago via the *Endosymbiotic Theory*—larger prokaryotic species engulfed smaller ones that continued to live and function within the larger host cell. Eventually, the mitochondria and chloroplasts were the two organelles created from these smaller cells, resulting in a eukaryotic cell.

7. Prior to 500 million years ago, life was confined to aquatic environments. Plants eventually found a foothold on earth (root system) via a symbiotic relationship with fungi.

B. The Early Atmosphere

1. Primitive earth was thought to have the following atmospheric molecules—water (H_2O), methane (CH_4), hydrogen (H_2), and ammonia (NH_3). No oxygen.

2. *Miller-Urey Experiment*—tested the Oparin-Haldane model that the atmosphere on primitive earth was the precursor for the synthesis of organic molecules.

       i. The primitive atmosphere components when given electric spark eventually formed crude organic molecules including sugars, lipids, amino acids, and nucleic acids.

      ii. *Heterotrophic Hypothesis*—first forms of life were prokaryotic heterotrophs that used non-biologically produced organic matter, via the Oparin-Haldane model, as their carbon source. *Still no oxygen produced.*

C. RNA—The First Genetic Material

  1. RNA was most likely a self-replicating molecule found in aquatic environments.

  2. RNA can self-catalyze its synthesis via its *ribozyme (RNA enzyme)* capability.

  3. Eventually, DNA became the genetic material, because of its stability over RNA and ability to correct mutations.

D. Current Models for the Origins of Prokaryotic and Eukaryotic Cells

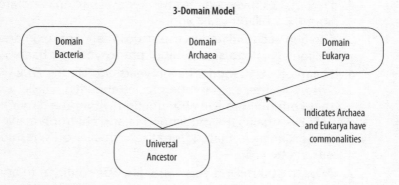

3-Domain Model

Domain Bacteria

Domain Archaea

Domain Eukarya

Indicates Archaea and Eukarya have commonalities

Universal Ancestor

  1. Carl Woese developed a *domain level* that is more inclusive than the Kingdom system.

  2. Universal Ancestor—primordial organism that was unicellular, anaerobic, prokaryotic, used ATP for energy and DNA as the genetic material.

  3. Bacteria and archaea are both at the prokaryotic level, but archaea live in more harsh conditions than bacteria.

Types of Archaea
Methanogens—produce methane and are used to convert waste to CH_4.
Acidophiles—thrive under highly acidic conditions.
Halophiles—thrive under high salt conditions.
Thermophiles—thrive under high temperature conditions.

4. When comparing archaea to eukarya, they have much in common with each other (more than bacteria). Examples include several types of RNA polymerase, introns, ribosome structure, RNA sequence, and non-response to antibiotics.

E. Early Prokaryotic Characteristics

1. Origination—around 4 billion years ago
2. Anaerobic fermentation (glycolysis)—primary metabolic pathway
3. Used organic compounds made via *Oparin-Haldane Model— Heterotrophic Hypothesis*
4. Eventually chemoautotrophs were selected because of their ability to make energy when the environment had been depleted for ATP.
5. *Cyanobacteria (blue-green algae)*—photosynthetic bacteria that were able to produce oxygen.

F. Early Eukaryotic Characteristics

1. Earliest eukaryotic descendents of prokaryotes were *Protists*.
2. Diverse unicellular organisms.
3. Motile, having cilia and flagella.
4. Can be photoautotrophs or heterotrophs.
5. *Endosymbiotic Theory*—Larger prokaryotic species engulfed smaller ones that continued to live and function within the larger host cell. Eventually, the mitochondria and chloroplasts were the two organelles created from these smaller cells, resulting in a eukaryotic cell. Developed by Lynn Margulis.

Evidence for Endosymbiotic Theory

Mitochondria and chloroplasts have DNA similar to prokaryotic DNA (sequence and shape are circular).

Mitochondria and chloroplasts are double membrane and double bound, similar to prokaryotes.

Mitochondria and chloroplasts are similar in size to prokaryotes.

Mitochondria and chloroplasts have their own ribosomes like prokaryotes.

Mitochondria and chloroplasts reproduce via binary fission like prokaryotes.

Test Tip

***Heredity and Evolution**—Being able to clearly identify the characteristics of early prokaryotes has been a hallmark of all AP Biology tests.*

Evidence for Evolution

I. Evidence for Evolution

A. Early Theories

1. In the 1700s and 1800s, the biological sciences were defined in terms of *natural theology*, rather than scientific data and extrapolation. Several scientists began to use data to debunk natural theology as a means for explaining scientific findings.

2. *Carolus Linnaeus*—founder of taxonomy or the classification of organisms based on anatomical similarities and differences. Developed the binomial system or *Genus species, ex. Homo erectus.*

3. *Georges Cuvier*—developed paleontology or the study of fossils found in sedimentary rock. Coined the term *catastrophism*—strata in sedimentary rock was reflective of a catastrophic event that took place.

4. *James Hutton*—used the geologic concept of *gradualism*—major change in geology is a slow and ongoing process.

5. *Charles Lyell*—used the geologic concept of *uniformitarianism*—that the earth was shaped entirely by slow-moving forces still in operation today, acting over a very long period of time

6. *Thomas Malthus*—indicated that populations could grow so rapidly, they could outgrow their food supplies.

7. *Jean Baptiste Lamarck*—developed *Lamarckism*—traits can be inherited from one generation to the next via the process of "the inheritance of acquired characteristics." For example, a giraffe's neck gets longer with each successive generation or a good baseball player can pass his traits to his children. There is no evidence, however, to prove this theory that

an "acquired characteristic" can be passed to the next generation. Another name for this is *use and disuse*; if a trait is used it will be passed down to the next, but, if not used, it will be discarded and not passed along. His theory was still considered visionary because of its emphasis on adaptation to the environment.

B. Descent with Modification—The Darwinian World

1. English scientist Charles Darwin voyages on the HMS *Beagle* to explore the South American coastline.

2. On the Galapagos Islands he found 12 different types of finches that were similar, but each had unique characteristics.

3. Darwin made a link between the origin of a new species and the environment in which these species reside.

4. The *theory of natural selection* is coined—reproductive success of an organism depends on its ability to adapt to the environment in which it resides. For example, several of the finches in the Galapagos Islands adapted their beak structure in order to find food.

5. Postulates of natural selection—

   i. If the environment cannot support the individuals who occupy it, then most of the offspring will perish.

   ii. Survival of individuals within a population will depend on the genetic background of the individual. Individuals with the best traits will survive. Another name for this is the "survival of the fittest."

   iii. Over time, the fittest organism will survive and therefore changes in the population will take place to benefit the reproduction of the population.

   > The result of natural selection is the adaption of populations to their environment, thus giving them a competitive advantage to survive.

   iv. Below is a classic example of natural selection (hypothetical data). The graph indicates that as time changes, the average beak length of a finch changes depending on the season. During a dry season the average beak length gets slightly larger, giving the finches a better advantage to transverse terrain and outcompete other birds for seeds that are less abundant in a wet season. A larger beak indicates a competitive advantage and survival of the fittest. Dry seasons are 1950 and 1980; wet seasons are 1960, 1970, 1990, and 2000.

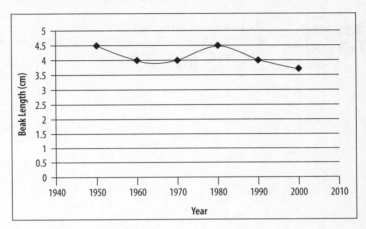

C. Evidence for Evolution

1. *Biogeography*—study of organisms and how they relate to the environment. Organisms may be unique to certain geographies that are present in one particular location. Hence, the organism has adapted to live in that environment.

2. *Fossils*—help indicate the progression of organisms from simple to complex. For example, transitional fossils are fossils of animals that display a trait that helped the organism attain a competitive advantage. At one time whales had limb-like fossils indicating they may have been land dwellers at one time.

3. *Comparative Anatomy*—study of anatomical similarities between organisms. *Homologous structures*—structures with organisms that indicate a common ancestor. For example, a human arm, cat leg, whale flipper, and bat wing all have a similar structure, but different functions. *Vestigial organs*—remnants of structures that were at one time important for ancestral organisms.

4. *Comparative Embryology*—comparing the embryonic development of one organism to another.

5. *Molecular Biology*—used in the study of evolution by looking at homology in DNA and protein sequences. See chart in Chapter 3 on cytochrome proteins. This is the best evidence that can be used when studying the relationships of species.

Test Tip

Heredity and Evolution—*Darwinian biology permeates all aspects of biology. Knowing the evidence of evolution and early theories of evolution can make up a series of questions on the AP Biology exam.*

Mechanisms of Evolution

I. Mechanisms of Evolution

A. Population Genetics

1. *Population Genetics*—study of genetic variation within a population of individuals.
2. *Population*—a group of individuals that belong to the same species.
3. *Gene Pool*—the total sum of genes within a population at a given time.
4. *Hardy-Weinberg*—study of the gene pool of a non-evolving population.
5. Hardy-Weinberg can only be met if the following five conditions are met:
   i. No mutation
   ii. No gene flow or genetic variation
   iii. A very large population sample
   iv. No natural selection
   v. Random mating
6. Mathematical Relationship of Hardy-Weinberg—equation that can help you determine whether a population is in Hardy-Weinberg equilibrium
   i. p = represents the frequency of the dominant allele
   ii. q = represents the frequency of the recessive allele
   iii. Assume a population of 500 pea plants in which green is dominant to yellow.

A = green, a = yellow

Phenotype	Green	Green	Yellow
Genotype	AA	Aa	aa
Number of pea plants (total = 500)	320	160	20
Genotypic frequencies	320/500 = 0.64 AA	160/500 = 0.32 Aa	20/500 = 0.04 aa
Number of alleles in gene pool	320 x 2 = 640 A	160 A & 160 a	40 a
Allelic frequencies	800/1000 = 0.8A p = frequency of A = 0.8	200/1000 = 0.2a q = frequency of a = 0.2	

➤ $p + q = 1$ (combined gene frequency must be 100%)
➤ $p^2 + 2pq + q^2 = 1$
   • p^2 = frequency of AA genotype = 0.8 × 0.8 = 0.64 = 64%
   • $2pq$ = frequency of Aa genotype = 2 × 0.8 × 0.2 = 0.32 = 32%
   • q^2 = frequency of aa genotype = 0.2 × 0.2 = 0.04 = 4%

7. Sample AP Biology Problem Using Hardy-Weinberg (Know this concept . . . it is always on AP tests):

   Assume that in a population of insects, body color is being studied. 36% represent the orange color which is recessive to 64% which represent the black dominant phenotype.

   > If each successive generation maintains the allele frequency, the population is said to be in Hardy-Weinberg equilibrium.

   1) Determine the allelic frequencies.
   2) Determine the genotypic frequencies.

   • The recessive phenotype is key to this problem because the dominant represents both AA and Aa. However, recessive is ONLY represented by aa. Use logic that q^2 = aa, therefore the square root of .36 or q = 0.6. Since $p + q = 1$, p + 0.6 = 1, then p = 0.4.

- Allelic frequencies are A = 0.4, a = 0.6.
- Genotypic frequencies follow the equation
  $p^2 + 2pq + q^2 = 1$.
- $p^2 = 0.4^2 = 0.16 = 16\%$
  (AA or homozygous dominant) → Black phenotype
  $2pq = 2 \times 0.6 \times 0.4 = 0.48 = 48\%$
  (Aa or heterozygous) → Black phenotype
  $q^2 = 0.6^2 = 0.36 = 36\%$
  (aa or homozygous recessive) → Orange phenotype
  $16 + 48 + 36 = 100$

B. Microevolution

1. *Microevolution*—defined as evolution on small scale from one generation to the next.
   i. *Genetic Drift*—changes in the gene pool due to chance because of a small population. The small population directly contrasts the large population needed to maintain Hardy-Weinberg equilibrium.
   ii. *Bottleneck Effect*—changes in the gene pool due to some type of disaster or massive hunting that inhibits a portion of the population from reproducing. The small population directly contrasts the large population needed to maintain Hardy-Weinberg equilibrium.
   iii. *Founder Effect*—a new colony is formed by a few members of a population. The smaller the sample size, the less the genetic makeup of the population. The small population directly contrasts with the large population needed to maintain Hardy-Weinberg equilibrium.
   iv. *Gene Flow*—transfer of alleles from one population to another through migration. The gametes of fertile offspring mix within a population, providing genetic variation. Genetic variation directly contrasts the no-gene-flow postulate needed to maintain Hardy-Weinberg equilibrium.
   v. *Mutation*—a change in the genetic makeup of an organism at the DNA level. Mutation directly contrasts the no mutation postulate needed to maintain Hardy-Weinberg equilibrium.
   vi. *Non-random Mating*—individuals mating with those in close vicinity. Non-random mating directly contrasts with

the random mating postulate needed to maintain Hardy-Weinberg equilibrium.

vii. *Natural Selection*—reproductive success of organisms depends on their ability to adapt to the environment in which they reside. Natural selection directly contrasts with the no natural selection postulate needed to maintain Hardy-Weinberg equilibrium.

C. Modes of Natural Selection

1. Natural Selection will favor the allelic frequency in three ways. Below is an example of a bell curve or normal distribution population. Three types of selections can take place that shift the bell curve to different frequencies (hence, evolution is taking place).

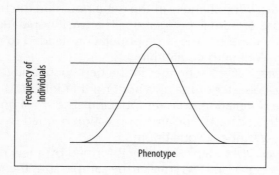

Original frequency of individuals shows a normal "bell-curve" distribution

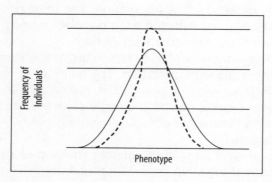

Stabilizing Selection—Extreme phenotypes are removed and more common phenotypes are selected

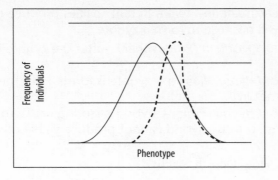

Directional Selection—One of the extreme phenotypes is selected

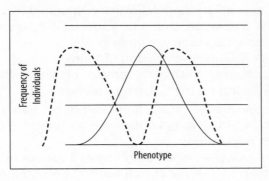

Diversifying Selection—Both of the extreme phenotypes are selected

D. Macroevolution

1. *Macroevolution*—evolution that forms new taxonomic groups.

2. *Speciation*—the origin of new species (a population of individuals who can mate with each other and produce viable offspring).

3. *Barriers to Speciation (Pre-zygotic)*—before the zygote is formed.
   i. *Habitat Isolation*—two species may live in the same area, but have a different habitat. One may be tree dwelling, while another may be terrestrial.
   ii. *Behavioral Isolation*—two species may display totally different behaviors that do not attract each other for mating.
   iii. *Temporal Isolation*—two species may breed at different times of the day or different seasons.
   iv. *Mechanical Isolation*—two different species may be anatomically different.

        v. *Gametic Isolation*—two different species produce gametes that will not fuse to form a zygote.

    4. *Barriers to Speciation (Post-zygotic)*—after the zygote is formed.

        i. *Reduced Hybrid Viability*—zygote is formed but the zygote does not live.

        ii. *Reduced Hybrid Fertility*—hybrid offspring are born and mature, but the hybrid cannot produce viable offspring.

E. Speciation—How Does It Occur?

    1. *Allopatric Speciation*—populations are separated by geographical isolation, thus a new species can be formed following adaption to new surroundings.

        i. *Adaptive Radiation*—Evolution of a large number of species from a common ancestor. Examples of this are the finches Darwin found on the Galapagos Islands.

    2. *Sympatric Speciation*—populations are not separated by geographical isolation, but a new species is formed amongst the parent populations.

        i. *Autopolyploidy*—meiotic error causes a species to have more than two sets of chromosomes. Contribution is from one species.

        ii. *Allopolyploidy*—polyploidy is a result of two different species.

F. Speciation—How Fast Does It Occur?

    1. *Gradualism*—species are produced by slow evolution of intermediate species.

    2. *Punctuated Equilibrium*—speciation happens quickly at first and then is followed by small changes over a long period of time.

Heredity and Evolution—Do you like math? Let's hope so because there may be easy mathematical calculations on the AP Biology test. For example, you should know how to appropriately use the Hardy-Weinberg equation: $p + q = 1$, $p^2 + 2pq + q^2 = 1$. Also make sure you understand how to use the chi-square equation—don't memorize it. If needed, it will be given to you: $X^2 = \Sigma \left[\dfrac{(o - \theta)^2}{\theta} \right]$.

PART IV:

ORGANISMS AND POPULATION:
Diversity of Organisms, Structure and Function of Plants and Animals, Ecology

Evolutionary Patterns

I. Evolutionary Patterns of Animals

A. Body Plans of Animals

1. *Phylum Porifera*—represent sponges. Lack true tissues and do not have nervous, digestive, or circulatory systems. Many Porifera are sessile or attached to some type of environment.

2. *Phylum Cnidaria*—represent hydra, jellyfish, and sea anemones. These organisms have radial symmetry. *Radial symmetry* indicates the organism has a top (*dorsal end*) and a bottom (*ventral*), but no left or right. *Bilateral symmetry*— organism has dorsal, ventral, *anterior* (head), and *posterior* (tail). Phyla included are *Platyhelminths* (flatworms), *Rotifera* (rotifers), *Nematoda* (nematodes), *Mollusca* (clams, snails), *Annelida* (segmented worms), *Arthropoda* (crustaceans, insects, spiders), *Echinodermata* (sea urchins), and *Chordata* (vertebrates).

   i. *Cephalization*—all bilateral organisms have this process associated with them. Anterior region of organism contains sensory paraphernalia. This will allow for the development of the central nervous system (brain and extending nerve cord). Bilateral organisms need to move, crawl, burrow, or even walk, which indicates the salient need for a CNS.

B. Germ Layers

1. *Gastrulation*—the process of layering the embryo into three germ layer regions *(triploblastic)*. Phylum Cnidaria are diploblastic; all others are triplobastic.

      i. *Ectoderm germ layer*—outer part (ecto-) of the germ layer and produces central nervous system, the lens of the eye, ganglia and nerves, the epidermis, hair, and mammary glands.

     ii. *Endoderm germ layer*—innermost part (endo-) of the germ layer and produces the stomach, the colon, the liver, the pancreas, the urinary bladder, the intestines, the lining of the urethra, the epithelial parts of the trachea, the lungs, the pharynx, the thyroid, and the parathyroid.

   iii. *Mesoderm layer*—middlemost part (meso-) of the germ layer and produces skeletal muscle, the skeleton, the dermis of the skin, connective tissue, the urogenital system, the heart, blood, and the spleen.

C. Body Cavities

  1. *Coelom*—a body cavity completely lined with mesodermic tissue allowing the organs to grow independent of a body wall (thus allowing regulation of one-organ system not affecting another). Having a coelom also allows for larger body size and cushioning and protecting internal body parts. A coelom is a true evolutionary advantage for an organism.

      i. *Coelomates* have a true coelom. Phyla include Mollusca, Annelida, Arthropoda, Echinodermata, and Chordata.

     ii. *Acoelomates* completely lack a coelom. Phylum includes Platyhelminthes.

   iii. *Pseudocoelom*—a body cavity that is only partially lined by mesodermic tissue. Phyla include Rotifera and Nematoda.

D. The Coelomate Dichotomy

  1. *Protostomes*—coelomate phylum that includes Mollusca, Annelida, amd Arthropoda.

      i. *Spiral Cleavage and Determinate Cleavage of Embryonic Cell*—causes small cells to be adjacent to larger cells at the 8-cell stage. Determinate cleavage at this point indicates the cells at this stage form an inviable embryo if separated from one another.

ii. *Coelom Formation*—coelom forms from splits in the mesoderm.

iii. *Blastopore* (opening of archenteron or primitive gut system)—mouth develops from blastopore

2. *Deuterostome*—coelomate phylum that includes Echinodermata and Chordata.

i. *Radial Cleavage and Indeterminate Cleavage of Embryonic Cell*—causes all cells to be aligned with each other at the 8-cell stage. Indeterminate cleavage at this point indicates the cells at this stage form a viable embryo if separated from one another.

ii. *Coelom Formation*—coelom forms from folds of the archenteron.

iii. *Blastopore* (opening of archenteron or primitive gut system)—anus develops from blastopore

Organisms and Population—*The topic of evolutionary patterns of animals eludes many students during studying. This topic is worth 2-3 questions on the AP Biology test. Be sure you know it!*

Survey of the Diversity of Life

I. Survey of the Diversity of Life

A. Representative Organisms of Domain Bacteria Kingdom Monera

1. Unicelluar, prokaryotic, with no nucleus.
2. No membrane-bound organelles
3. Archaea—"ancient bacteria." See chapter 21.
4. *Eubacteria*—true bacteria.
    i. Have specialized cell wall made up of peptidoglycan (protein and sugar).
    ii. *Gram-negative* bacteria stain pink because of complex cell wall.
    iii. *Gram-positive* bacteria stain purple because of less complex cell wall.
    iv. *Decomposers*—feed on dead or decaying organisms.
    v. *Nitrogen fixation*
    vi. *Coccus*—spherical shape.
    vii. *Bacillus*—rod shape.
    viii. *Spirillum*—spiral shape
    ix. *Endospore*—protective layer formed by bacteria that protects them from harsh conditions such as heat, pressure, or lack of food.
5. Common Eubacteria
    i. *Escherichia coli or E.coli*—intestinal pathogen.
    ii. *Streptococcus pneumoniae*—causative agent of bacterial pneumonia.
    iii. *Bacillus anthracis*—soil dwelling and causative agent of anthrax.
6. How Eubacteria Gain Energy
    i. *Photoautotroph*—use photosynthesis or light energy to make carbon sources.

    ii. *Chemoautotroph*—need carbon dioxide for carbon source, but inorganic molecules for energy.

    iii. *Photoheterotroph*—use light energy to make ATP, but need carbon from an outside source.

    iv. *Chemoheterotroph*—consume organic molecules for energy and carbon.

B. Representative Organisms of Domain Eukarya Kingdom Protista

  1. Most diverse of all eukaryotes.

  2. Unicelluar or multicelluar.

  3. *Protozoans*—animal-like protists.
    i. Amoeba
    ii. Algae

  4. *Unicellular algae*—plant-like protists.
    i. Euglena
    ii. Dinoflagellates
    iii. Diatoms

  5. *Motion classification*
    i. *Amoeba*—move by a false foot or pseudopodia.
    ii. *Ciliates*—move via cilia.
    iii. *Flagellates*—move via flagella.

C. Representative Organisms of Domain Eukarya Kingdom Fungi

  1. Yeast (unicellular) or multicellular.

  2. *Saprobes*—derive their nutrition from nonliving organic material.

  3. *Lichens*—symbiotic relationship between fungus and cyanobacterium.

  4. Produce antibiotics that work against prokaryotic cells. The best example of this is *Penicillium chrysogenum*, or fungus that produces the antibiotic penicillin.

D. Nine Major Animal Phyla

  1. Phylum Porifera
    i. Sponges.
    ii. Invertebrates that have a porous body, thus they are filter feeders.

iii. Anchored to a stratum.

iv. Radial symmetry.

2. Phylum Cnidaria

    i. Hydra, sea anemone, jellyfish (tentacle-containing organisms).

    ii. Invertebrates that have a true gastrovascular cavity (mouth).

    iii. Radial symmetry.

3. Phylum Platyhelminthes (planaria)

    i. Flatworms.

    ii. Invertebrates that a have a true gastrovascular cavity (mouth).

    iii. Bilateral symmetry.

    iv. Simple nervous system and first organisms to have cephalization.

4. Phylum Nemotoda

    i. Nemotodes or round worms (parasitic).

    ii. Invertebrates with a complete digestive tract (mouth and anus).

    iii. Bilateral symmetry.

5. Phylum Annelida

    i. Invertebrates.

    ii. Segmented worms such as the earthworm or leech.

    iii. Bilateral symmetry.

6. Phylum Mollusca (mollusks)

    i. Very diverse phylum of invertebrates.

    ii. Clams, snails, squid, octopi, scallops.

    iii. Major parts of all mollusks

        a. *Visceral mass*—organ-containing system

        b. *Head-foot region*—head for sensory function, and foot for motor function.

        c. *Mantle*—secretes the shell.

        d. *Radula*—sharp tongue for eating.

7. Phylum Arthropoda

    i. Phylum containing the most number of animals because of insect class.

    ii. Invertebrates

    iii. Major parts of all arthropods.

        a. They have a so-called *exoskeleton* or hard outer covering that supports and protects muscles.

        b. Jointed appendages.

        c. Segmented body.

8. Phylum Echinodermata
   i. Invertebrates that include sea stars and sea urchins.
   ii. Radial symmetry.
   iii. Spiny skin, an *endoskeleton*, and a water vascular system for food and waste transportation.
9. Phylum Chordata
   i. Most chordates are vertebrates, but not all.
   ii. Major parts of all chordates.
      a. Notochord that supports the back.
      b. Dorsal hollow nerve cord.
      c. Pharyngeal gill slits for feeding.
      d. Post-anal tail.

E. Chordate Classes

1. Class Osteichthyes
   i. Bony fish
   ii. Gill formation for breathing
   iii. *Operculum*—flap above gill that allows the fish to breathe without moving.
2. Class Amphibia
   i. First terrestrial vertebrates
   ii. Limb development for movement
   iii. Cold-blooded
   iv. Lay eggs in water
   v. Gills replaced by lungs
3. Class Reptilia
   i. Scales for waterproofing.
   ii. Terrestrial amniotic egg. There are four extra embryonic membranes that are adaptations of the terrestrial egg: *chorion* contributes to the formation of the placenta; *amnion sac* cushions the embryo; *yolk sac* provides nourishment for the egg; and *allantois* collects waste materials and exchanges gases from the embryo.
   iii. *Ectothermic*—warm bodies via heat from environment.
4. Class Aves
   i. Wings, feather, and hollow light bones for flying.

5. Class Mammalia
   i. Warm blooded and four-chambered heart.
   ii. *Endothermic*—warm blooded.
   iii. Hair and mammary glands.
   iv. Development of offspring within mother prior to live birth.

F. Major Plant Divisions

1. Division Bryophyta—Non-vascular seedless plants.
   i. Moss, liverworts, hornworts.
   ii. Grow in moist conditions because of lack of vascular system.
   iii. Flagellated sperm that require water so they can swim to the egg.
   iv. Gametophyte is dominant life cycle.
2. Division Pteridophyta—Vascular seedless plants.
   i. Ferns
   ii. Spores born on underside of leave.
   iii. Sporophyte is dominant life cycle.
3. Phylum Coniferae—vascular seed plants
   i. Called gymnosperms.
   ii. Douglas Fir, Cedar, and other woody plants.
   iii. Cone-bearing plants.
   iv. Sporophyte is dominant life cycle
4. Phylum Anthophyta—vascular seed plant.
   i. Called angiosperms or flowering plants.
   ii. Formation of flower allowed for co-evolution with other organisms.
   iii. Sporophyte is dominant life cycle

Test Tip

Organisms and Population—*The terrestrial amniotic egg was a major evolutionary adaption for birth to happen outside of water.*

Phylogenetic Classification

I. Diversity of Organisms—Phylogenetic Classification

A. Taxonomy—Classification of Organisms

1. Developed by Carolus Linnaeus and based on similarity of organisms.
2. Hallmark is binomial nomenclature or genus species (*Homo sapien*).

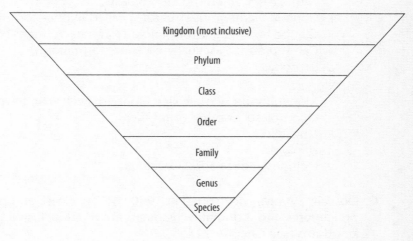

Kingdom (most inclusive)

Phylum

Class

Order

Family

Genus

Species

B. Major Kingdoms

1. Animalia
   i. Animals are multicellular with organ systems.
   ii. Cells have organelles including a nucleus, but no chloroplasts or cell walls.

          iii. Move with the aid of cilia, flagella, or muscular organs.

          iv. Heterotrophic—must ingest other organisms for sustenance.

  2. Plantae

     i. Plants are multicellular with organelles including chloroplasts and cell walls.

     ii. Nutrients are acquired by photosynthesis (autotrophic).

  3. Protista

     i. Protists are single-celled organisms.

     ii. Move by cilia, flagella, or by amoeboid mechanisms.

     iii. There is usually no cell wall, although some forms may have a cell wall.

     iv. May have chloroplasts.

     v. Nutrients are acquired by photosynthesis, ingestion of other organisms, or both (autotrophic and heterotrophic).

  4. Fungi

     i. Fungi are multicellular (except yeast, which are unicellular), with a cell wall but no chloroplasts.

     ii. Contain filamentous structures called hyphae for growth.

     iii. Can be haploid and/or diploid (some have stages of both).

     iv. Can reproduce asexually via spore formation.

     v. Saprobic.

  5. Monera

     i. Monerans are single-celled, contain a cell wall, have no chloroplasts or other organelles.

     ii. Nucleoid.

     iii. Haploid.

     iv. Include Archaea and Eubacteria.

C. Domain System—developed in 1990 by Carl Woese and places prokaryotes into 2 domains. Domains are more inclusive than kingdoms (see Chapter 21).

  1. Domain Bacteria

     i. Kingdom Monera

  2. Domain Archaea

     i. Kingdom Monera

3. Domain Eukarya
   i.   Kingdom Protista
   ii. Kingdom Fungi
   iii. Kingdom Plantae
   iv. Kingdom Animalia

> **Organisms and Population**—*The domain system of classification is fairly new when compared to the kingdom system. Even though the domain system is more inclusive, test questions can be derived from both forms of classification.*

Evolutionary Relationships

I. Diversity of Organisms—Evolutionary Relationships

A. Sedimentary Rocks

1. *Fossil record*—strata that are formed are based on time. Top strata contained the most recent fossil record, while bottom strata contain older fossils.

B. Molecular Biology

1. *Protein comparison*—homology of the primary amino acid structure.
2. *DNA and RNA comparisons*
   i. *DNA-DNA hybridization*—measuring the extent of hydrogen bonding between DNA of two different sources.
   ii. *Restriction Enzyme Mapping*—restriction enzymes recognize and cut sequences of DNA. A pattern can be observed using DNA gel electrophoresis.
   iii. *DNA sequence analysis*—comparing nucleotide sequence.

C. Cladistics

1. A clade is a group of organisms that includes an ancestor and *all* descendents of that ancestor. Cladistics is based on molecular techniques (DNA and RNA sequences) rather than morphology or form and structure of animals.

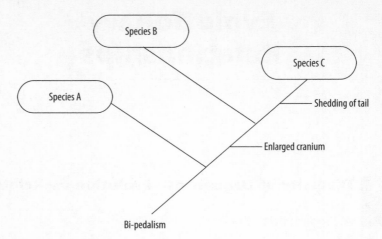

Species B

Species C

Species A

Shedding of tail

Enlarged cranium

Bi-pedalism

➤ Species B and C are more closely related to each other than to species A.
➤ All species are generated from an ancestor species with bi-pedalism.
➤ All species retain traits from the ancestor but have evolved to gain some specific trait through time.

Organism	Bi-pedal	Large Cranium	Tail Loss
Species A	X		
Species B	X	X	
Species C	X	X	X

Plants and Animals— Reproduction, Growth, and Development

I. Reproductive Process of All Land Plants

A. Alternation of Generations

    1. Two main multi-cellular forms called gametophyte and sporophyte.

    2. Gametophyte is haploid and produces the egg and sperm.

    3. Sporophyte is diploid formed by the fusion of egg and sperm.

    4. Meiosis produces the spore that will eventually give rise to sporophytes via mitosis.

    5. Fertilization of male and female gametophyte produce a sporophyte.

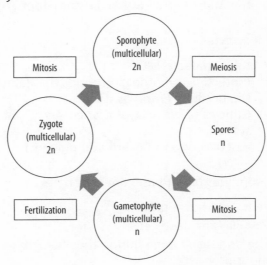

II. The Rise of Land Plants

A. Green Algae

　1. Gave rise to land plants.

　2. Most live in fresh water, but there are some marine (not a land plant).

　3. No vascular tissue or root system.

B. Bryophytes

　1. Moss, liverworts, hornworts.

　2. None vascular and seedless.

　3. Have no root system, but are anchored via *rhizoids* or non-vascular containing cells.

　4. The dominant stage during the lifecycle of bryophytes is the gametophyte.
　　i. *Antheridia*—produces the male gametophyte
　　ii. *Archegonia*—produces the female gametophyte
　　iii. Fertilization takes place in the archegonia. Water droplets are required to transport male gametophyte to archegonia.
　　iv. *Sporangium* produces spores that will eventually produce the mature male or female gametophyte.

C. Tracheophytes

　1. 4 major characteristics
　　i. Protective layer that surrounds the gametes.
　　ii. Multicellular embryos.
　　iii. Cuticles or waxy layer that covers all parts above the root system.
　　iv. Vascular system (xylem and phloem)

D. Pteridophytes (most basic tracheophytes)

　1. Ferns and horse tails.

　2. Vascular and seedless.

　3. The dominant stage during the life cycle of pteridophytes is the sporophyte.

      i. Antheridia—produces the male gametophyte.

     ii. Archegonia—produces the female gametophyte.

  4. Water droplets are required to transport male gametophyte to archegonia.

  5. Sporangia are found on the underside of the leaf and produce spores that will undergo fertilization.

E. The Seed

  1. Allows for protection.

  2. Seed = sporophyte embryo along with a food source.

  3. Seed can remain dormant but viable until favorable conditions are met.

  4. Dispersal via wind or animals.

F. Gymnosperm—conifers or cone-bearing plants such as pine.

  1. The dominant stage during the life cycle of gymnosperms is the sporophyte.

  2. *Ovule*—structure containing the eggs that are produced via meiosis.

  3. *Pollen Cone*—pollen grains (haploid) are produced via meiosis.

  4. *Ovulate Cone*—contains two ovules.

  5. *Pollen Grain*—2 male gametophytes formed via pollination land on ovulate cone. One will be destroyed while the other will wait at least one year before fertilization takes place.

  6. Once a new embryo (only 1 of the eggs is fertilized) is produced (sporophyte), a seed coat will be produced and the unfertilized female gametophyte will become the food reserve.

G. Angiosperm—flowering plant.

  1. The dominant stage during the life cycle of angiosperms is the sporophyte.

  2. Reproductive structure of angiosperms is the flower.

     i.   *Sepal*—enclose and protect the flower before it buds.

     ii. *Petal*—bright-colored structure that attracts insects for pollination.

    iii. *Stamen*—male reproductive organ.

    iv. *Carpel (pistal)*—female reproductive organ.

    v. *Anther*—part of the stamen where pollen is produced via meiosis.

    vi. *Stigma*—part of the carpel; receives the pollen.

    vii. *Style*—part of the carpel that leads to the ovary.

    viii. *Ovary*—part of the carpel where the ovule is encased.

3. *Fruit*—a mature ovary.

    i. After fertilization, the ovary thickens to aid in protection.

    ii. Fruits aid in dispersing seeds because some are edible by other species. Once eaten, the seed's protective coat will not break down and the organism will pass the seed through feces at a distant location from where it was eaten. The feces also contain a plethora of fertilizer that will aid in germination.

4. Double fertilization and the endosperm

    i. In contrast to gymnosperms where one of the pollen grains is destroyed, both pollen grains fertilize one egg in angiosperms. This is called *double fertilization*.

    ii. The triploid nucleus will continually divide giving rise to a rich food reserve called the *endosperm*.

    iii. *Cotyledon* or seed leaves are produced. Monocots produce 1 seed leaf while dicots produce 2 seed leaves.

> ***Organisms and Population**—Be sure to know the four main plant groups: bryophytes, seedless vascular plants, gymnosperms, and angiosperms. The gametophyte is the dominant generation of bryophytes, while the sporophyte is dominant in seedless vascular plants. In seed plants, such as gymnosperms and angiosperms, the seed replaces the spore as the main means of dispersing offspring.*

III. Animal Reproduction

A. Various Types of Reproductive Patterns

1. *Asexual reproduction*—no genetic diversity since all genes come from one parent. No fusion of egg and sperm.

    i. *Budding*—outgrowths from a parent form and pinch off to live independently.

    ii. *Binary Fission*—a type of cell division by which prokaryotes reproduce; each daughter cell receives a single parental chromosome.

    iii. *Fragmentation*—breaking of a body piece that will form an adult via regeneration of body parts.

  2. *Sexual reproduction*—genetic diversity since genes will be inherited from both parents. Fusion of egg and sperm.

  3. *Parthenogenesis*—egg develops without being fertilized.

  4. *Hermaphroditism*—having both male and female reproductive organs.

B. Spermatogenesis (happens in gonads)

  1. Continuous throughout the life of a male.

  2. 4 viable sperm produced via meiosis in the testes.

C. Oogenesis (happens in ovary)

  1. After first meiotic division cytokinesis is unequal with the secondary oocyte receiving all of the cytoplasm from the oogonium.

  2. At birth the ovary contains all cells that will develop into the egg.

  3. Only 1 viable ovum is produced with 3 non-viable polar bodies.

D. The Reproductive Cycle of the Human Female

  1. Menstrual cycle or changes in the uterus or female reproductive organ.

  2. 28-day cycle in which the destruction and regeneration of the uterine lining (endometrium) occurs.

    i. *Menstrual Phase* (day 0-5)—menstruation (bleeding due to destruction of endometrium).

    ii. *Proliferative Phase* (day 6-14)—regeneration of endometrium.

    iii. *Secretory Phase* (day 15-28)—endometrium becomes more vascularized and is ready for implantation of embryo. If the embryo is not implanted, the entire menstrual cycle will happen again.

3. *Ovarian Cycle*—parallels the menstrual cycle.
   i. *Follicular Phase* (day 0-13)—egg cell enlarges in a follicle.
   ii. *Ovulation* (day 14)—oocyte is released and pregnancy can take place.
   iii. *Luteal Phase* (days 15–30)—the corpus luteum is formed. A structure that grows on the surface of the ovary where a mature egg was released at ovulation. The corpus luteum produces progesterone in preparing the body for pregnancy.

4. Important hormones
   i. *Gonadotropin-releasing hormone*—aids in the release of FSH and LH.
   ii. *Luteinizing hormone (LH)*—stimulates ovaries.
   iii. *Follicle-stimulating hormone (FSH)*—stimulates production of ova (ovulation) and corpus luteum.
   iv. *Estrogen*—stimulates uterine lining growth.
   v. *Progesterone*—stimulates uterine lining growth.

IV. Animal Development

A. Fertilization

1. Process of egg and sperm fusion to make a zygote.
2. Activation of egg that will lead to embryonic development.

B. After Fertilization

1. *Cleavage*—a series of rapid cell divisions to form *blastomeres (blastula)* or small cells with their own nucleus.
2. Cleavage is the succession of rapid cell divisions without growth during early embryonic development which converts the zygote into a ball of cells.
3. When the blastomere reaches the 16-32 cell stage, it is called a *morula*.
4. The morula will then become a gastrula by gastrulation. The gastrula will form the three embryonic tissues of the ectoderm, endoderm, and mesoderm.

Plants—Structural, Physiological, and Behavioral Adaptations

 I. **Structure and Function of Plants—Structural, Physiological, and Behavioral Adaptations**

A. Diversity of Angiosperms

1. Monocots and dicots

Part	Monocot	Dicot
Embyro	One cotyledon (mono)	Two cotyledons (di)
Leaf Venation	Parallel	Net like
Stems	Complex arrangement of vascular bundles	Ring arrangement of vascular bundles
Roots	Fibrous root	Taproot
Flowers	Flowers in multiples of 3	Flowers in multiples of 4 or 5

B. Cell Types

1. *Parenchyma cells*—perform the metabolic processes of cells.
2. *Collenchyma cells*—support the plant.
3. *Sclerenchyma cells*—rigid cells that are found in areas where the plant is no longer growing.

C. Tissue Types

1. Vascular-xylem tissue
   i. Type of vascular tissue that transports water and dissolved minerals from the roots up the plant.

      ii. *Tracheids and vessel elements*—dead cells that conduct water and minerals.

  2. Vascular-phloem tissue

      i. Type of vascular tissue that transports food from the leaves to the roots of the plant.

      ii. *Sieve-tube members*—live cells, but have no organelles. Main function is to transport sucrose.

      iii. *Companion cells*—next to sieve-tube member and provide all the metabolic resources for the sieve tube members.

> Xylem works *upward*; Phloem works *downward*!!!

  3. Dermal Tissue—protects the plant.

      i. *Cuticle*—waxy coat that helps the plant retain water.

  4. Ground Tissue—occupies space between vascular and dermal tissues

      i. Mostly made up of parenchyma cells.

D. Plant Growth

  1. *Apical meristems or primary growth*—located at the tips of roots or shoot buds and contain the cells undergoing mitosis for vertical or expansive cell growth.

  2. *Lateral meristems or secondary growth*—located through the length of the shoot system and roots and is considered outward horizontal growth (increases plant's diameter).

Test Tip

***Organisms and Population**—Memorize! Memorize! Memorize! Do not lose points because you forgot the properties of plant cells and tissues.*

Animals—Structural, Physiological, and Behavioral Adaptations

Structure and Function of Animals—Structural, Physiological, and Behavioral Adaptations

A. Mammalian Digestive System

   1. Oral Cavity (only carbohydrates are broken down)
      i. Mouth secretes *salivary amylase* which breaks down starch. Chewing or mechanical digestion is also carried out. *Bolus* or ball of food is formed.
      ii. *Pharynx,* or back of the throat, has a structure called the epiglottis that blocks food from going down the windpipe or trachea.
      iii. *Esophagus*—food tube that conducts bolus down to the stomach via a smooth muscle contraction called *peristalsis.*

   2. Stomach (only protein is broken down)
      i. *Gastric Juice*—a digestive fluid with pH of about 2 that aids digestion.
      ii. *Pepsin*—a protease secreted in an inactive form called pepsinogen until food is present in the stomach.
      iii. *Acid Chyme*—food and gastric juice that is processed in the stomach.

   3. Small Intestine and Accessory Organs (all 3 macromolecules are broken down)
      i. Organ that digests most food and absorbs it into the blood.
      ii. *Duodenum*—first part of the small intestine where digestion takes place.
      iii. *Pancreatic enzymes* are sent to the small intestine to aid in digestion. These enzymes are protease, amylase, and lipase. *Bile* from the liver (stored in the gallbladder)

emulsifies or opens up the fat for lipase to break it down. Fat is broken down for the first time in the small intestine.

iv. *Microvilli* of the small intestine increase the surface area and allow for absorption of nutrients.

4. Large Intestine or Colon (No Digestion)
    i. Main purpose is for reabsorption of water.
    ii. Feces are created and eliminated through the rectum or end of the large intestine.

B. Circulatory System

1. *Open Circulatory System*—blood mixes with internal organs directly. Insects, arthropods, and mollusks have an open circulatory system.

2. *Closed Circulatory System*—blood is confined to blood vessels that lead to the organs. Earthworms, octopi, and vertebrates have a closed circulatory system.

3. Fish—one ventricle, one atrium with gill capillaries allowing for gas exchange.

4. Amphibian—one ventricle and two atrium; have lung and skin capillaries for gas exchange. Have *double circulation* or oxygen-rich blood going to the organs and oxygen deficient blood returning to the right atrium.

5. Mammal—two ventricles and two atrium, with lung capillaries for gas exchange. Also makes use of double circulation.

6. Flow of Blood in Mammalian Heart
    i. Deoxygenated blood from the vena cava enters the right atrium and passes through the right atrioventricular valve (tricuspid valve) into the right ventricle. From the right ventricle it travels out of the heart via the pulmonary artery where it becomes oxygenated at the lungs (CO_2 is exchanged for O_2). Oxygenated blood then travels via the pulmonary vein to the left atrium and through the left atrioventricular valve (mitral or bicuspid valve) into the left ventricle. Oxygenated blood then leaves the left ventricle of the heart via the aorta to the organs of the body.

7. Beating of the Heart
    i. Cardiac muscle transfers an electrical signal via the following: Sinoatrial (SA) node or "pacemaker" of the

heart (top of right atrium) generates an electrical impulse that is relayed to the atrioventricular (AV) node located between the right atrium and right ventricle. The signal then transfers to the bundle branches and Purkinje fibers at the heart's apex.

8. Blood Pressure
    i. The force of blood against a blood vessel wall is a measure of blood pressure.
    ii. *Systolic pressure* is peak pressure in the arteries, which occurs when the ventricles are contracting. *Diastolic pressure* is minimum pressure in the arteries, which occurs when the ventricles are filled with blood. The ratio of systolic and diastolic pressure is the measurement of blood pressure (systolic pressure/diastolic pressure).

C. Respiratory System

1. Gas exchange is defined as the uptake of oxygen (O_2) and loss of carbon dioxide (CO_2).
2. *Gills*—specialized for gas exchange of aquatic organisms.
3. *Tracheal system and lungs*—specialized for gas exchange of terrestrial organisms. For an insect such as a grasshopper, the tracheae opens to the outside.
4. *Lungs*—Amphibians (frogs) are the only vertebrates that use skin along with lungs to promote gas exchange.
5. Flow of Air in Mammalian Lungs
    i. Inhaled air passes through the *larynx* (upper part of the respiratory tract) into the *trachea or windpipe* (rings of cartilage). The trachea divides into two *bronchi* leading to the lungs. The bronchi branch to *bronchioles* which contain air sacs called *alveoli*. The alveoli are covered with capillaries where the gas exchange will take place.
6. Control of Breathing
    i. *Medulla oblongata*, lower part of the brainstem, maintains homeostasis by monitoring CO_2 levels. When CO_2 levels are high, the CO_2 reacts with water in the blood, dropping the pH of the blood. The medulla oblongata senses a pH drop and excess CO_2 is exchanged for O_2.
7. Hemoglobin
    i. Iron—containing protein of mammalian red blood cells.

D. Immune System

1. First Line of Defense (non-specific)
    i.   Skin
    ii. Mucous
2. Second Line of Defense (non-specific)
    i.   Inflammatory Response
    ii. Antimicrobial Proteins
3. Third Line of Defense (specific)
    i.   Lymphocytes (T and B cells)
    ii. Antibodies
4. Immune Response
    i.   *Primary Immune Response*—first exposure to antigen (foreign molecule) requires 10-15 days for lymphocytes to generate the maximum response.
    ii. *Secondary Immune Response*—second exposure to antigen requires less time to react to antigen. The response is greater and longer. This response is based on immunological memory that the immune system retains after the primary exposure.

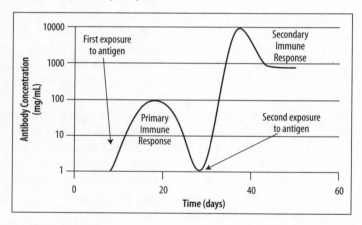

5. Self vs. Non-self
    i.   One of the hallmarks of the immune system is to distinguish self from non-self. Immune cells and other body cells coexist in a state known as self-tolerance.
6. Passive and Active Immunity
    i.   *Active Immunity*—immunity gained by recovering from a disease. Can also be gained from *vaccination* (immunization).

  ii. *Passive Immunity*—immunity gained by one individual passing antibodies to another.
7. Antibody Structure
  i. Y-shaped proteins that bind antigens at specific antigenic determinants called epitopes.

  ii. 5 types of antibodies:
   ➤ *IgG*—most abundant antibody, crosses the placenta and gives passive immunity to fetus.
   ➤ *IgA*—present in body secretions such as saliva and tears.
   ➤ *IgM*—first antibody in the primary immune response.
   ➤ *IgD*—found on the cell surface of B cells
   ➤ *IgE*—released in response to allergic attacks.

E. Control Systems

 1. Thermoregulation
  i. *Body Insulation*—hair, feathers, and fat reduce heat loss.
  ii. *Vasodilation*—increased blood flow to the skin, causing heat loss.
  iii. *Vasoconstriction*—decreased blood flow to the skin, reducing heat loss.
  iv. *Cooling*—sweating or panting.
  v. *Behavorial*—organism can move to a warmer or colder region.
  vi. *Hibernation*—decreased body temperature because of decreased metabolic activity.

F. Urinary (Excretory) System

 1. *Malpighian Tubules*—excretory organs of insects and arthropods.
 2. *Mammalian Kidney*—bean-shaped organ (mammals have 2).

      i. Blood enters the kidney via the *renal artery* and leaves the kidney via the *renal vein.*

      ii. Urine leaves the kidney and enters the bladder via the *ureter.*

      iii. Urine in the bladder is excreted via the *urethra.*

      iv. *Renal medulla*—inner portion of the kidney

      v. *Renal cortex*—outer portion of the kidney

3. *Nephron*—basic structural and functional unit of the kidney (roughly 1 million per kidney).

4. Nitrogenous Waste Products
   i. *Ammonia*—aquatic animal waste (very toxic and would be deadly for terrestrial animals).
   ii. *Urea*—mammalian and amphibian waste that breaks down to form ammonia.
   iii. *Uric Acid*—birds, snails, insects, and reptiles.

5. Production of Urine
   i. *Glomerulus*—renal artery becomes a ball of capillaries surrounded by a *Bowman's Capsule* within the nephrons of the kidneys, which collects fluids (filtrate) as they pass through the glomerulus.
   ii. The filtrate will pass through *proximal tubule, loop of Henle,* and *distal tubule.*
   iii. Urine is gathered in the *collecting duct,* where it empties into the urinary bladder via the ureter.

G. Nervous System

1. *Central Nervous System (CNS)*—brain and spinal cord.

2. *Peripheral Nervous System (PNS)*—all other nervous system structures outside the CNS.

3. *Neuron*—basic unit of nervous system.
   i. *Cell Body*—large portion of neuron that contains the nucleus and organelles.
   ii. *Dendrites*—communicate the nervous signal from tips of neuron to the cell body.
   iii. *Axon*—conduit that communicates down the neuron away from the cell body.
   iv. *Myelin Sheath*—lipid-based insulation around the Schwann cells that stops the leaking of the nervous signal.

      v. *Schwann Cell*—chain of cells that propagates the nervous signal.
     vi. *Node of Ranvier*—space or gap between the Schwann cells.
    vii. *Synapse*—the space between the end of the axon and the target; examples of targets include muscles or other neurons.

4. Passage of a Nerve to a Reflex Action
      i. Signal → Sensory Receptor → Sensory Neuron → Interneuron → Motor Neuron → Muscle
     ii. *Presynaptic Membrane*—surface of synaptic terminal that faces the synaptic cleft. Neurotransmitter (packaged in a vesicle) will be released across the cleft to a postsynaptic cell via the presynaptic membrane.
    iii. *Postsynaptic Membrane*—surface of the cell body/axon that is on the opposite side of the synapse. Will receive the neurotransmitter and depolarization of the neuron will take place, thus propagating the signal.

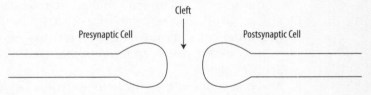

    Cleft

Presynaptic Cell   Postsynaptic Cell

5. Action Potential—the threshold required to be reached in order for an all or none change in the membrane potential of a neuron to occur
      i. All neurons have a charge associated with them because of the concentration of various ions being transported into and out of the cell. A cell at rest has a *resting membrane potential* of approximately $-70mV$. Both Na^+ and K^+ channels are closed.
     ii. *Depolarization*—reduction in the absolute value of membrane potential because Na^+ channels open and flood inside of the cell. K^+ channels are closed.
    iii. *Action Potential*—if depolarization hits the *threshold*, an action potential will be created. This is the example of the *all or none event*.
    iv. *Repolarization* and *hyperpolarization*—decrease in membrane potential (more negative) because K^+ channels

open and K⁺ leaves the cell. Na⁺ channels are closed. Returns the membrane potential from positive (caused by depolarization) to negative.

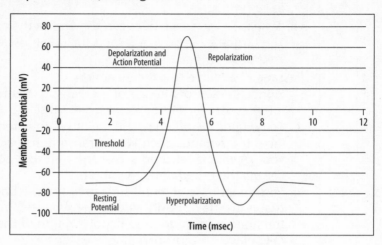

6. *Neurotransmitters*—chemicals that are released at synapses.
   i. *Acetylcholine*—can be inhibitory or excitatory. When the target cell is a muscle, then it is usually excitatory. *Acetylcholinesterase* is an enzyme that destroys acetylcholine.
   ii. *Norepinephrine* and *Epinephrine*—involved in flight or fight response and generally excitatory.
7. Parts of the brain
   i. *Medulla oblongata*—controls breathing, circulatory system, and digestive system.
   ii. *Pons*—accessory portion of brain that controls breathing.
   iii. *Cerebellum*—controls movements and coordination, i.e., hand-eye coordination.
   iv. *Cerebrum*—part of the forebrain and regulates the conscious functions of the body such as thought and reasoning and perception of stimuli.
   v. *Cerebral cortex*—key role is memory.
   vi. *Corpus callosum*—facilitates communication between the right and left hemispheres of the brain.
   vii. *Hypothalamus*—regulates body temperature, hunger, and thirst.

H. Endocrine System

1. Major Glands and Tissue
   i.   *Hypothalamus*—links the nervous and endocrine systems by receiving signals and propagating the endocrine response. Located in the lower half of the brain.
   ii. *Pituitary gland*—"master gland"; many of the hormones released by the pituitary gland communicate with other glands. The pituitary is under control of the hypothalamus.
   iii. *Thyroid gland*—located near the trachea.
   iv. *Parathyroid gland*—located on surface of the thyroid.
   v.   *Pancreas*—near the kidneys and contains specialized cells called Islets of Langerhans that secrete hormones.
   vi. *Adrenal gland*—located on top of the kidneys.
   vii. *Gonads*—testes and ovary.
   viii.*Pineal gland*—small peanut-shaped gland near the center of the brain.
   ix. *Thymus*—located in the upper portion of the chest cavity.

Gland	Hormone	Action
Pituitary	Oxytocin	Contraction of uterus; breast milk let-down
Pituitary	Antidiuretic hormone	Water retention in kidney
Pituitary	Growth Hormone	Stimulates growth
Pituitary	Prolactin	Stimulates milk production from mammary gland
Pituitary	Follicle Stimulating Hormone	Stimulates production of ova and sperm
Pituitary	Luteinizing Hormone	Stimulates ovaries

(continued)

Gland	Hormone	Action
Pituitary	Thyroid Stimulating Hormone	Stimulates the thyroid
Thyroid	Triiodothyronine (T_3) and thyroxine (T_4)	Stimulates metabolism
Thyroid	Calcitonin	Lowers calcium level in bloodstream; stimulates bone construction
Parathyroid	Parathyroid Hormone	Raises blood calcium
Pancreas	Insulin	Lowers blood glucose
Pancreas	Glucagon	Raises blood glucose
Adrenal Gland	Norepinephrine and Epinephrine	"Fight or Flight" response; stimulates metabolism
Testes	Androgens	Promote sperm formation and secondary male characteristics
Ovaries	Estrogens	Stimulate uterine lining and secondary female characteristics
Ovaries	Progesterone	Stimulate uterine lining growth; maintains pregnancy
Pineal	Melatonin	Sleep-wake cycle and other circadian rhythms

I. Sliding Filament Model of Muscle Contraction

1. Interaction of two proteins called *myosin* and *actin*.
2. Myosin binds to actin and simultaneously ATP will be hydrolyzed.

3. An interaction between myosin and actin causes the actin filaments to be moved (sliding) and muscle contraction to take place.

4. Ca^{2+} ions are essential ions needed for the entire process to take place.

Test Tip

***Organisms and Population**—All the systems of the body come together to maintain the homeostasis of the body. This is a central theme in the AP Biology curriculum.*

Plants—Response to the Environment

I. Structure and Function of Plants—Response to the Environment

A. Transport of Water and Minerals in Plants

1. *Water Potential* ψ—combination of both solute concentrations and pressure. Water will always flow from a high water potential to a lower water potential.

2. Equation for water potential $\psi = \psi_{presssure} + \psi_{solute}$

3. *Plasmodesmata*—channels between plant cells that allow the flow of fluids.

4. Flow of water in roots begins at the *root hair* or extensions of the epidermal cells.
   i. From the root hair water will travel to the epidermis, cortex, the endodermis, and stele which contain xylem cells.
   ii. *Casparian strip*—a waxy lipid found in the endodermis that repels water and forces it into the stele.

5. *Mycorrhizae*—symbiotic relationship between plant roots and fungus that assists the plant in transferring water.

B. Transpiration

1. *Transpiration*—loss of water through the plant leaf.

2. *Xylem sap*—water and dissolved inorganic ions that ALWAYS flow from the roots of the plant to the leaves.

3. *Guttation*—xylem sap that can be found as droplets on leaves.

4. *Root Pressure*—forcing of water up the xylem as a result of water entering the root system via osmosis. Guttation is the main result of root pressure.

5. *Transpiration—Cohesion-Tension Model*
   i. Water is taken up by the root system of the plant (transpiration).
   ii. Cohesion of water molecules to each other and the adhesion of water to the cell wall start the ascent of water up the plant (cohesion).
   iii. The top of the plant has a lower water potential than the bottom of the plant. Water travels up the plant based on the water potential gradient.
   iv. As more water leaves the plant leaf via transpiration, the water potential becomes more negative (this is called tension) driving even more xylem sap up the plant.
6. Regulation of Transpiration
   i. *Guard cells*—open and close the *stomata* of the cell, which changes the amount of gas exchange and water loss.

C. Translocation

1. *Translocation*—transport of food (phloem sap) in the plant via phloem.
2. *Sink-Source Model*
   i. *Source Cell*—cell that produces sucrose via photosynthesis. These are mesophyll cells, which are found in the leaf.
   ii. *Sink Cell*—cell that will consume or store sugar. These cells are roots, stems, and fruits.
   iii. Sugar from the source is loaded into the sieve tube members and is transported down the phloem via pressure flow.
   iv. Phloem sap will reach the sink cells where sucrose will be transported into the sink. The water that assisted to transport the sucrose will be recycled to the xylem cell and move up the xylem.

D. Plant Hormones

1. *Auxin*—stimulates stem elongation, development of fruit, and root growth.
2. *Abscisic acid*—inhibits growth.

3. *Ethylene*—promotes the ripening of fruit.
4. *Cytokinins*—stimulated cell division, growth, and germination.
5. *Gibberellic acid*—stimulates the flowering of a plant and the development of fruit.

E. Tropisms

1. *Phototropism*—plant growing toward light. Main hormone that allows this is auxin.
2. *Gravitropism*—growing in response to gravity. Positive gravitropism is exhibited by roots since they grow downwards. Shoot systems of plants exhibit negative gravitropism or growth against gravity.
3. *Thigmotropism*—directional growth of plants growing around structures, such as vines on walls.

F. Photoperiodism—response of a plant to the length of day and night (a circadian rhythm)

1. *Short-day (long-night) plant*—requires a longer amount of darkness to bloom. This type of plant will bloom when the amount of darkness exceeds the *critical night length*.
2. *Long-day (short-night) plant*—requires a shorter amount of darkness to bloom. This type of plant will bloom when the amount of darkness is less than the *critical night length*.

G. Phytochromes—pigments that plants use to detect light.

1. Phytochromes are sensitive to red and far-red light.
2. Red light promotes the growth of long-day plants, but inhibits short-day plant growth.
3. A burst of far-red light following red light can reverse the effects of the red light.

Test Tip

Organisms and Population—The sink-source model is a great example of structure and function with the key molecule being water.

Biosphere

I. Ecology—Biosphere

A. *Abiotic Factors*—non-living physical or chemical factors. Temperature, light, weather.

B. *Biotic Factors*—living factors. Organisms in an environment.

C. Levels of Ecological Organization—biosphere is more inclusive than individual.

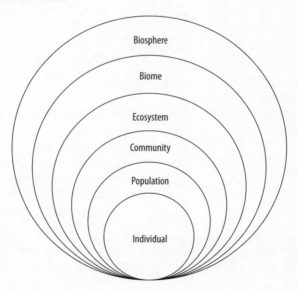

II. Terrestrial Biomes

Biome	Major Location	Features
Tropical Rain Forest	South America	• Tremendous organic diversity • High rainfall • Poor soil because of high rainfall • Canopy or topmost layer is made of trees that block sunlight • Slash and burn techniques commonly used • Very low temperature range
Desert	Northern Africa Southwest U.S. Australia	• Little rainfall • Cacti and other water-storing plants found (i.e., succulents) • Usually hot, but there are cold deserts (i.e., Antartican Desert) • No canopy • Plants are spiny for protection
Savanna or the tropical grassland	Central and South Africa	• Large herbivores • Dominant herbivores are insects • Grasses, patches of trees are major plants • Seasonal droughts with dry and wet seasons • Warm temperature year round
Chaparral	West coast of U.S.	• Known for wildfires • Sloping mountains with shrubs • Coastal area with hot, dry summers and mild, rainy winters

(continued)

Biome	Major Location	Features
Temperate Grassland	North American Prairies	• Grass is major plant • Nutrient rich soil for agricultural growth • Grazing by large animals • In the U.S., called farmland
Temperate Deciduous Forest	Northeast U.S.	• Deciduous—falling of leaves prior to winter • Hibernation for animals because of 4 true seasons • Hickory, oak, maple are major trees
Coniferous Forest or Taiga	Upper North America or Canadian Region	• Cone-bearing plants such as pine • Cold temperatures • Moose, bear, deer
Tundra	Upper North America or Canadian Region	• Permafrost or permanently frozen soil • Very little rainfall • Short growth season and little diversity • Moss and liverworts dominant plants (gymnosperms) • Too cold for reptiles or amphibians

III. Aquatic Biomes

A. Vertical Stratification

1. *Upper Photic Zone*—lots of light for photosynthesis.
2. *Lower Photic Zone*—low amount of light, therefore, little photosynthesis but some still occurs.
3. *Benthic Zone (Aphotic Zone)*—bottom of aquatic biomes. Benthos, or organisms that live at the bottom, feed on *detritus* or dead organic matter. No light penetrates.

B. Freshwater Biome

1. *Littoral Zone (part of Photic Zone)*—located where aquatic or root-based plants live. Close to shore.

2. *Limnetic Zone (part of Photic Zone)*—farther from shore where phytoplankton live.

3. *Profundal Zone (part of Aphotic Zone)*—deep Aphotic region.

C. *Wetland*—any area covered with water that supports aquatic growth. Can be flooded or have soil that is permanently saturated during the growing season.

D. *Estuary*—area where fresh and saltwater meet.

E. Marine Biome

1. *Intertidal Zone (part of Photic zone)*—where land meets water.

2. *Neritic Zone (part of Photic zone)*—shallow water regions.

3. *Oceanic Zone (part of Photic zone)*—past the continental shelf to far depths.

4. *Abyssal Zone (part of Aphotic zone)*—very deep benthic communities that are very cold and have total darkness, with no nutrients. No photosynthetic activity, therefore, primary productivity is low.

Test Tip

***Organisms and Population**—There is a multitude of information regarding biomes in this chapter. Any one of these facts could be in a multiple-choice question or be used as supporting evidence for an essay.*

Population Dynamics

I. Ecology—Population Dynamics

A. *Population Density*—number of people per unit area.

B. *Dispersion*—how individuals in a population are spaced per unit area.

  1. *Clumped*—individuals are aggregated in patches or groups.

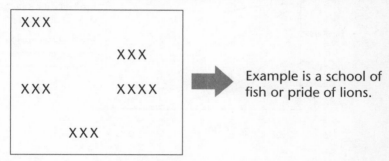

Example is a school of fish or pride of lions.

  2. *Random*—arbitrary pattern of individuals.

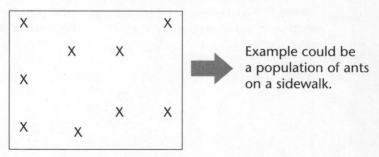

Example could be a population of ants on a sidewalk.

3. *Uniform*-pattern based, or evenly spaced individuals.

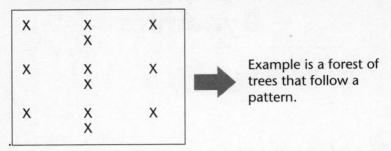

Example is a forest of trees that follow a pattern.

C. *Survivorship Curve*—simple graph of the number of individuals alive at certain ages.

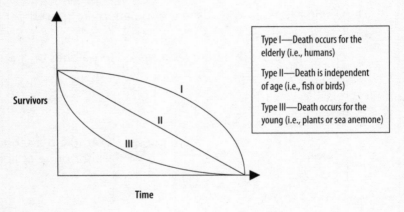

Type I—Death occurs for the elderly (i.e., humans)

Type II—Death is independent of age (i.e., fish or birds)

Type III—Death occurs for the young (i.e., plants or sea anemone)

D. *Population Growth Models*

1. *Exponential Model*—unlimited growth of the population because of no limitation on resources. The result is a *J-shaped curve*.

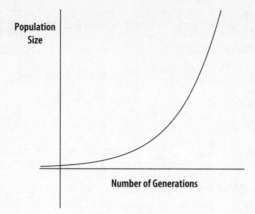

2. *Logistic Model*—limited growth of the population because of limited resources. The result is an *s-shaped curve*. The *carrying capacity* or the maximum population size that a habitat can hold (defined by the letter *K*).

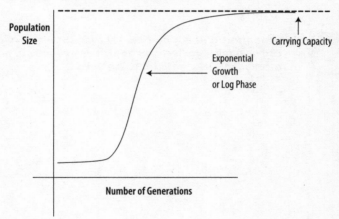

3. *K-selected population*—have a density near their resources or their carrying capacity. For example, humans.
4. *r-selected population*—a population that grows fast, reproduces fast, and dies rather quickly. For example, bacteria.

K-selected population	r-selected population
Slow sexual maturation	Rapid sexual maturation
Long life span	Short life span
Large offspring	Small offspring
Type I survivorship curve	Type III survivorship curve
Sexual reproduction	Asexual reproduction

5. *Density-dependent factors*—A factor that affects population size based on the density of population. Most likely biotic factors such as food, predation, migration, or disease.

6. *Density-independent factors*—A factor that affects the population size regardless of density. Most likely abiotic factors such as weather or natural disaster.

Test Tip

Organisms and Population—The logistic model of growth can be applied to bacterial growth as well as viral growth. It is commonly used with those examples.

Communities and Ecosystems

I. ***Population Interaction*—interactions that occur with different species living in a community (conglomerate of different species living in one location).**

A. *Predation*—predator eats the prey. One species benefits while the other does not.
1. *Adaptations for predator*—claws, teeth, poisons, speed, eyesight.
2. *Adaptations for prey plants*—thorns in plants, plant chemicals that ward off prey.
3. *Adaptations for animals*—cryptic coloration or camouflage, aposematic coloration or bright colors that warn, or warning noises.
4. *Mimicry*—prey resembles another species.
   i. *Batesian mimicry*—a harmless species mimics a species that is dangerous to the predator.
   ii. *Müllerian mimicry*—two harmful species resemble each other and create a cumulative effect against a predator.

B. *Parasitism*—parasite lives off the host. One species benefits while the other does not (i.e., viruses, tapeworms, and mosquitoes).

C. *Competitive Exclusion Principle*—two species cannot survive in the same *ecological niche* (the sum of the total abiotic and biotic factors in an ecosystem). Neither species benefits from this interaction.

D. *Symbiosis*—means living together between a host and a symbiont.

1. *Commensalism*—One species benefits while the other is not affected. An example is a clownfish that lives within a sea anemone's poison tentacles. The clownfish is protected and the sea anemone is neither harmed nor benefited.

2. *Mutualism*—Both species benefit from the interaction.
   i. Pollination between insects and plants.
   ii. Fungi and algae in lichen.
   iii. *Rhizobium*—bacteria living in the root nodules of plants supplying the organism with amino acids, while accepting carbon in the form of organic acids for respiration.
   iv. Bacteria living in the gut of a cow secrete the enzyme cellulase which helps break down cellulose for the cow. The bacteria have a comfortable place to live, and the cow receives nutrients from the broken-down cellulose.

3. *Coevolution*—the evolution of one species acting as a selective agent for the evolution of a second species. An example would be the co-evolutions of plants and insects.

II. *Ecological Succession*—Changes in the Composition of a Community Over Time.

A. *Primary Succession*—Area starts off containing lifeless conditions, such as a volcanic island or barren land. Initial *pioneer species,* such as moss and lichen, colonize the area. Fertile soil develops and grass, shrubs, and other plants begin to grow. This process can take hundreds of years.

B. *Secondary Succession*—Area has been destroyed by a natural disaster, farming, or slash-and-burn techniques. The area returns to its initial state because the fertile soil in the area has not been removed. This process can be completed within one year.

III. *Ecosystems*—All the Organisms Living in a Community, Including Abiotic and Biotic Factors.

A. *Trophic Levels*—division of organisms in an ecosystem.

1. *Primary Producers*—photosynthetic organism such as plants and blue green algae.
2. *Primary Consumers*—herbivores or plant-eating organisms.
3. *Secondary Consumers*—carnivores that eat the primary consumers.
4. *Tertiary Consumers*—carnivores that eat carnivores or organisms below them.
5. *Detritivores*—derive their energy from dead organisms or detritus (i.e., fungi and soil microbes). Extremely helpful in recycling matter.

B. *Food Chain*—pathway in which food is transferred from one trophic level to the next. Arrow points to the organism that is "doing" the eating.

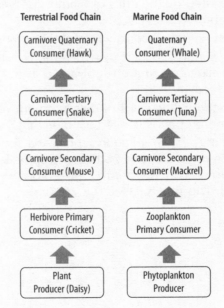

C. *Food Web*—an elaborate web of organisms feeding at more than one trophic level.

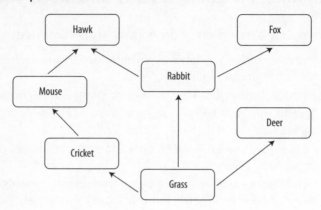

D. *Energy Flow in Ecosystems*

1. *Primary Productivity*—the amount of light energy converted to chemical energy in an ecosystem, by autotrophic organisms. Measured by the units of *biomass* or weight per unit area per unit time ($g/m^2/yr$).
2. *Gross Primary Productivity*—total primary productivity.
3. *Net Primary Productivity*—the energy used by producers for cellular respiration subtracted from the gross primary productivity.
4. *Secondary Productivity*—measurement of an organism's intake of energy that is converted to weight.
5. *Loss of Energy from a food chain*—each time energy is taken in by an organism at a particular trophic level, only 10% of that energy is converted into a new biomass for the next trophic level. This rule is called the *10% rule*.

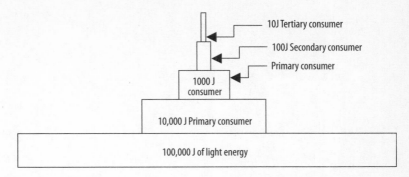

6. *Pyramids of Biomass*—because of the 10% rule, biomass pyramids tend to follow the same scheme and shape. Producers have the greatest biomass for the most part.

E. Cycling of Elements

1. *Water Cycle*—cycling of water through evaporation, precipitation, percolation, and runoff.

2. *Carbon Cycle*—cycling of carbon through photosynthesis and cellular respiration. Burning of fossil fuels is another source of carbon dioxide in the atmosphere, as is volcanic action.

3. *Nitrogen Cycle*—nitrogen enters the cycle as atmospheric nitrogen or through *nitrogen fixation*, or the conversion of nitrogen into compounds that can be used, such as amino acids or nucleic acids. Soil bacterium called *rhizobium,* found in the root nodules of plants, uses nitrogen fixation.

4. *Phosphorus Cycle*—Phosphorus from the weathering of rocks or soil is cycled around from one organism to another.

Organisms and Population—*You need to understand the differences between a food web and a food chain. A food chain is exactly that—a chain of organisms that feed on each other. A food web is more complex and actually indicates the relationship among several different organisms that may feed on one another.*

Ecology—Behavior

I. Ecology—Behavior

A. *Innate Behavior*—all organisms exhibit certain behaviors that are not learned, but are "built in." (For example, a baby holding onto its mother's hand when born.) Usually not changed by the environment.

B. *Fixed Action Pattern*—set of behaviors that cannot be changed. An example would be Nikolaas Tinbergen's digger wasp experiment in which the wasp located its nest based on markings and visual cues.

C. *Repertoire*—series of songs that can be distinguished by organisms and signal an action. Mostly done by birds for mating purposes.

D. *Learning*—modifying your behavior based on specific events in a lifetime.

E. *Habituation*—loss of response to stimulus. For example, if a certain animal hears the calls of a predator, but the predator does not attack, eventually it will no longer respond to the stimulus.

F. *Imprinting*—learning a behavior at a specific time in an organism's life. An example would be Konrad Lorenz's becoming the mother of young geese.

G. *Classical Conditioning*—learning associated with a reward or punishment. Pavlov's dog experiment: when the dogs heard the sound of a bell at feeding time, they started to salivate for food. Eventually, they were conditioned to salivate anytime they heard the bell, independent of food being present or not.

H. *Operant Conditioning*—learning by trial and error. B.F. Skinner's box experiment.

I. *Kinesis*—changing the rate of an action in response to a stimulus.

J. *Taxis*—movement away or toward a stimulus.

K. *Territoriality*—defending one's area, for example by marking the area and/or physical confrontation.

L. *Communication*—sending information from one organism to another (or group of organisms). Chemical communication can be done via pheromones or hormones that communicate mating. A classic example is the dancing of bees to communicate the location of food, discovered by Karl von Frisch.

M. *Altruism*—concern for the well-being of others or a group. This is most often seen in kin relationships.

N. *Hierarchy*—certain members of the group have a higher standing over other members. As a result, the members with a higher status feed before others, and have their choice of a mate.

O. *Group Size*—flocks, schools, herds, or prides can all be methods in which organisms organize themselves into groups. This allows for increased hunting efficiency as well as protection. However, the weaker members of the group may be subordinate to stronger ones. Communicable diseases can also have deleterious effects on the population numbers.

Test Tip

Organisms and Population—These terms may not seem to be part of a biology course, but behavior is a key evolutionary trait that will be tested on the AP Biology exam.

Ecology—Global Issues

I. Ecology—Global Issues

A. *Biological Magnification*—toxic chemicals being increased in concentration from one trophic level to the next. Biomass from one level is created from a larger biomass from the trophic level before. Top-level consumers are mostly affected. The best-known example is the use of DDT pesticide.

B. *Ozone Layer*—the ozone layer absorbs harmful UV light. CFCs or chlorofluorocarbons in aerosol cans and refrigeration units destroy the ozone by reducing it to oxygen.

C. *Greenhouse Effect*—carbon dioxide emissions from the burning of fossil fuels acts as a trap of solar heat in the atmosphere. Increases in carbon dioxide warm the air and accelerate the greenhouse effect. This is thought to be the major cause of global warming. Deforestation is also a major contributor to the greenhouse effect.

Test Tip

Organisms and Population—Environmental awareness is the hallmark to the homeostasis of biomes that are both terrestrial and marine.

PART V:
THE EXAM

Major AP Biology Themes and Their Relationship to the Exam

The AP Biology curriculum is unified by thematic underpinnings. These underpinnings can be related to any of the topics that are presented in this *AP Biology Crash Course*. A good way to utilize these themes is to incorporate them into your essays. The AP Biology readers will be delighted that you were able to see the big picture of the course, rather than small isolated concepts. Below are the major themes and some conceptual examples that apply to them.

I. Major Themes

A. Science as a Process

1. The experiments of Watson and Crick and others that lead to the discovery of DNA as genetic material;
2. The experiments of Gregor Mendel that lead to the basic laws of genetics;
3. The experiments of Thomas Hunt Morgan that lead to linked genes;
4. Miller-Urey experiment and its validation of the Oparin-Haldane model of the primitive atmosphere.

B. Evolution

1. Fermentation as the precursor for cellular respiration;
2. The Endosymbiotic Theory and the development of the eukaryotic cell;
3. The role of genetic variability in evolution: crossing over in meiosis, mutations, independent assortment of gametes;

4. The adaptations of various animal phyla and plant divisions.

C. Energy Transfer

1. Coupling of the four main processes of cellular respiration;
2. The coupling of cellular respiration and photosynthesis;
3. Hydrolysis of ATP in all 3 parts of the central dogma;
4. The utilization of energy in ecosystems.

D. Continuity and Change

1. The presence of carbon in all macromolecules as a means of continuity. However, the assimilation of carbon is different in carbohydrates, lipids, proteins, and nucleic acids;
2. Mitosis as a means of continuity and meiosis as a means of change;
3. The process of fertilization as a means of continuity throughout the domains of life, but the specialization of cells, tissues, and organs as a means of change after fertilization;
4. The overall structure of a biome is continuous while populations can change based on abiotic and biotic factors.

E. Relationship to Structure and Function

1. The differences between the structure of DNA and RNA leading to different cellular functions;
2. The homologous structures of body parts of organisms having different functions;
3. The various structured organ systems of the human body and their individual functions;
4. The structure of the genomes of eukaryotic and prokaryotic species leading to different cellular functions.

F. Regulation

1. The membrane as a means of selective permeability;
2. The function of inducers and repressors in an operon system;
3. The methods by which organisms that are ectothermic and endothermic regulate body temperature;

4. How various cycles such as water, carbon, and nitrogen maintain homeostatic levels.

G. Interdependence in Nature

1. The global issues that can disrupt an ecosystem;
2. The use of water in moss and fern fertilization;
3. Sunlight as the driving force of photosynthesis;
4. The survival of the fittest concept that drives evolution.

H. Science, Technology, and Society

1. The use of recombinant DNA techniques in all aspects of scientific inquiry;
2. Pollution in a technologically advanced society;
3. Global warming;
4. Deforestation results in overlapping ecological niches.

Test Tip

Themes—Use the themes to your advantage. If you mention these themes in your essay, the essay scorer will surely award you more points.

The 12 AP Biology Labs

Lab 1   Diffusion and Osmosis

	Initial Contents	Solution Color		Presence of Glucose	
		Initial	Final	Initial	Final
Bag	15% glucose & 1% starch	Clear	Blue/ black	Yes	Yes
Beaker	H_2O & IKI	Yellowish	Yellowish	No	Yes

Exercise 1A: Diffusion

• The interpretation of this exercise was that starch is too large a molecule to escape through the pores of the dialysis bag. As a result, the dialysis bag turns from clear to blue/black because the IKI from the beaker diffuses through the pores and reacts with the starch (a positive test for starch). The beaker fluid stays yellowish because no starch has diffused from the dialysis bag. Glucose is present in the beaker because it is a smaller molecule than starch and diffuses through the dialysis bag's pores. Residual glucose is still in the bag, thus you continue to have a positive result for the bag.

Exercise 1B: Osmosis

Contents in Bag	Percent Change
0.0 M Distilled Water	0.1%
0.2 M Sucrose	2.7%
0.4 M Sucrose	5.0%
0.6 M Sucrose	8.1%
0.8 M Sucrose	11.0%
1.0 M Sucrose	14.1%

% Change in Mass vs. Concentration of Sucrose

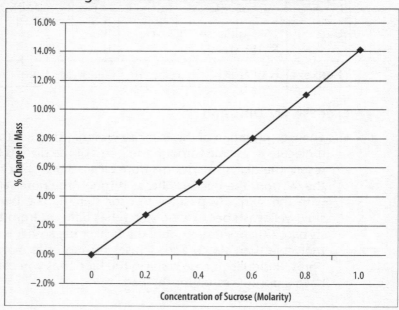

- The interpretation of this exercise was that as the concentration of the solute increased, water will diffuse into the dialysis bag (hypotonic to hypertonic), increasing the mass of the dialysis bag. An isotonic solution is evident with distilled water (diffusion is happening at equal rates into and out of the dialysis bag).

Contents in Beaker	Percent Change
0.0 M Distilled Water	19.0%
0.2 M Sucrose	8.0%
0.4 M Sucrose	– 5.0%
0.6 M Sucrose	–13.0%
0.8 M Sucrose	–21.0%
1.0 M Sucrose	–27.0%

Exercises 1C and 1D: Water Potential

% Change in Mass vs. Concentration of Sucrose

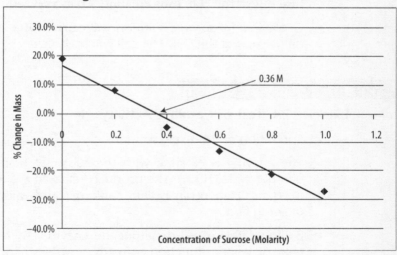

- The interpretation of this exercise indicates that when the line crosses the *x*-axis at 0.36 M (estimation) that is the concentration when the potato core would be isotonic to the sucrose concentration. A net change of 0% at *x* = 0.36 M is the concentration that the water potential in the potato tissue is equal to the sucrose concentration (isotonic).

- Calculation of water potential:

$$\psi_s = iCRT = -(1)\left(.36\frac{moles}{liter}H_2O\right)\left(0.0831\frac{literbar}{mole°K}\right)(295°K) = -8.8 \text{ bars}$$

If the calculated water potential is less than the water potential surrounding the bag, water will flow into the bag (more solute molecules inside the bag). If the calculated water potential is greater than the water potential surrounding the bag, water will flow out of the bag (less solute molecules inside the bag). Thus, water will flow from a high to low water potential.

Exercise 1E: Onion Cell Plasmolysis

- Interpretation of this exercise:

  ➤ Onion cell in hypotonic solution will cause water to diffuse into the cell, thus creating a turgid cell.

  ➤ Onion cell in hypertonic solution will cause water to diffuse out of the cell, thus creating a plasmolyzed cell.

  ➤ Onion cell in isotonic solution will cause water to equally diffuse across the cell. The cell will be flaccid.

Lab 2 Enzyme Catalysis

Exercise 2A: Test of Catalase Activity

- Interpretation of this exercise:

  ➤ The enzyme is catalase with the substrate being hydrogen peroxide (H_2O_2). The products released are water and oxygen. Oxygen gas is flammable gas and will reignite a glowing flint.

  ➤ Boiling catalase will denature the enzyme; therefore, the enzyme will not function correctly.

Exercises 2B, 2C, and 2D: Enzyme Catalyzed Reaction

	Time (seconds)						
	10	30	60	90	120	180	360
a) Base Line	5.6	5.6	5.6	5.6	5.6	5.6	5.6
b) Final Reading	10.1	14.4	15.6	15.8	15.8	15.8	15.8
c) Initial Reading	7.1	12.3	14.2	15.0	15.7	15.7	15.7
d) Amount of $KMnO_4$ Consumed	3.0	2.1	1.4	0.8	0.1	0.1	0.1
e) Amount of H_2O_2 Used	2.6	3.5	4.2	4.8	5.5	5.5	5.5

Amount of H_2O_2 Used vs. Time

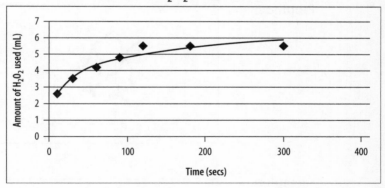

Lab 3   Mitosis and Meiosis

Exercise 3A.1: Observing Mitosis in Plant and Animal Cells Using Prepared Slides of Onion Root Tip and Whitefish Blastula

- The interpretation of this exercise:
  - ➤ Visually be able to draw a cell in Interphase (non-dividing portion of the cell cycle) and the 4 stages of mitosis.

Interphase

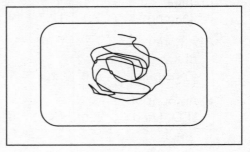

Prophase

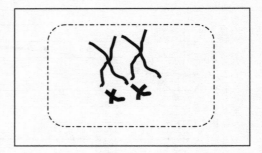

Metaphase

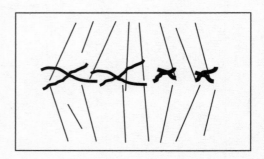

Anaphase

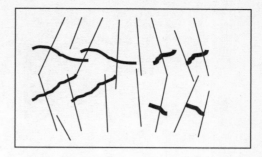

Telophase

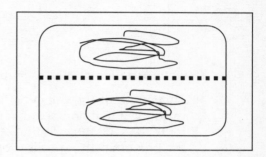

Exercise 3A.2: Time for Cell Replication

	Number of Cells				Percent of Total Cells Counted	Time in Each Stage
	Field 1	Field 2	Field 3	Total		
Interphase	500	600	700	1800	82.0%	19 hr 41 min
Prophase	50	60	70	180	8.2%	1 hr 58 min
Metaphase	30	40	50	120	5.5%	1 hr 30 min
Anaphase	15	20	30	65	3.0%	43 min
Telophase	8	10	12	30	1.3%	19 min
				2195		

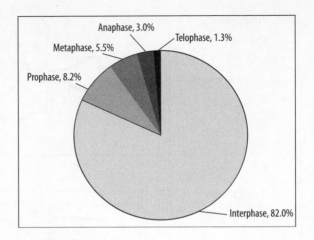

- The interpretation of this exercise:

  ➤ The length of the cell cycle is roughly 24 hours with the majority of that time spent in Interphase, getting prepared for mitosis. Of the cells that one would observe in mitosis, the predominant phase is prophase.

Exercise 3B.1: Meiosis

- The interpretation of this exercise:

  ➤ You must know the differences between meiosis and mitosis.

	Mitosis	Meiosis
Number of Chromosomes	2n-diploid	2n-diploid
Number of DNA Replications	1	1
Number of Divisions	1	2
Number of Daughter Cells Produced	2	4
Number of Chromosomes	2n-diploid genetically identical	n-haploid genetically variable
Purpose/Function	Growth of somatic cells	Generation of gametes

Exercise 3B.2: Crossing Over during Meiosis in *Sordaria fimicola*

- The interpretation of this exercise:

  ➤ The number of asci observed that show crossing over are called recombinants. Recombinants are progeny that do not resemble the genetic make-up of the parent.

  ➤ *Sordaria fimicola* is a fungus that after undergoing meiosis, another mitotic event will take place. This is unique to many fungi including *Saccharomyces cerevisiae* or baker's yeast.

  ➤ The crossing-over event that took place is depicted below. The different combinations result in how the haploid cells arranged themselves in the ascospore.

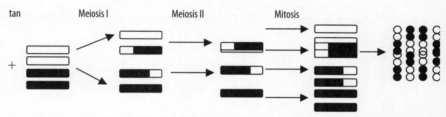

| | | tan | Meiosis I | Meiosis II | Mitosis |

Number of 4:4	Number of Asci Showing Crossing Over	Total Asci	% Asci Showing Crossing Over	Gene Distance
156	165	318	156/318 = .49 0.49/2 = 24.5%	24.5 map units

Lab 4   Plant Pigments and Photosynthesis

Exercise 4A: Plant Pigment Chromatography

- The interpretation of this exercise:

  ➤ The various plant pigments that help to run the photo-synthetic machinery can be separated out based on solubility in the solvent being used. The molecules involved in this are chlorophyll a, chlorophyll b, carotenoids, and xanthophylls. The relationship between the distance the pigments travel in relation to the solvent is calculated by a factor called R_f.

$$R_f = \frac{\text{distance pigment migrated}}{\text{distance solvent front migrated}}$$

Band Number	Distance (mm)	Band Color
1	10	yellow green
2	23	blue green
3	33	yellow
4	49	deep yellow
5	105	yellow

Distance of solvent front 122 mm

105/122 = 0.86	R_f for carotene (yellow to yellow orange)
49/105 = 0.46	R_f for xanthophyll (yellow)
23/105 = 0.22	R_f for chlorophyll a (bright green to blue green)
10/105 = 0.095	R_f for chlorophyll b (yellow green to olive green)

Exercise 4B: Photosynthesis/The Light Reaction

Cuvette	0 minutes	5 minutes	10 minutes	15 minutes
2/Unboiled Dark	22.1	22.4	22.4	22.5
3/ Unboiled Light	22.1	44.2	56.7	62.4
4/ Boiled Light	22.1	22.3	22.3	22.3
5/ No chloroplast light	22.1	22.3	22.3	22.4

- The interpretation of this exercise:

  ➤ The only combination in which the light reaction of photosynthesis will take place is in cuvette 2 since it has unboiled (functioning chloroplasts) with light. All other cuvettes either have destroyed chloroplasts or no light to start the light reaction. The artificial electron acceptor, called DPIP, that was used in the experiment is blue and replaces NADP. Once DPIP accepts the electrons from the light reaction, it turns from blue to clear, thus % transmittance increases using the spectrophotometer.

  ➤ **% Transmittance vs. Time (min)**

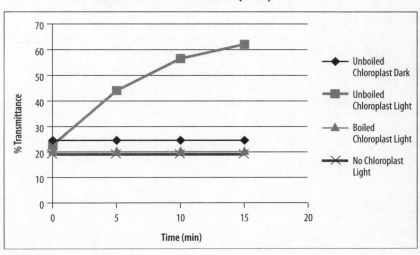

Lab 5　Cell Respiration

Exercise 5A: Measurement of O_2 Consumption

- The interpretation of this exercise:
  - ➤ Cell respiration takes place at both 30°C and 10°C for germinating peas (peas consume oxygen). The rates are linear and therefore can be calculated using the points in the data table. Germinating peas respire better (consume oxygen) at a higher temperature, because the enzymes of cell respiration move faster and have better kinetics at 30°C. Dry peas are not germinating, thus do not consume oxygen.

Temp (°C)	Time (min)	Beads Alone Reading at x	Beads Alone Difference	Germinating Peas Reading at x	Germinating Peas Difference	Germinating Peas Corrected difference	Dry Peas and Beads Reading at x	Dry Peas and Beads Difference	Dry Peas and Beads Corrected difference
30	0	0.90	X	0.90	X	X	0.90	X	X
	5	0.90	0	0.83	0.07	0.07	0.90	0	
	10	0.90	0	0.77	0.13	0.13	0.90	0	0
	15	0.90	0	0.70	0.20	0.20	0.90	0	0
	20	0.90	0	0.63	0.27	0.27	0.90	0	0
10	0	0.90	X	0.90	X	X	0.90	X	X
	5	0.90	0	0.87	0.03	0.03	0.90	0	0
	10	0.90	0	0.84	0.06	0.06	0.90	0	0
	15	0.90	0	0.81	0.09	0.09	0.90	0	0
	20	0.90	0	0.78	0.12	0.12	0.90	0	0

Oxygen Consumption (mL) vs. Time (min)

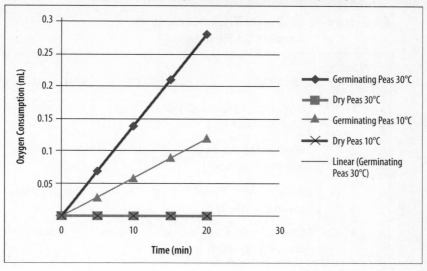

Condition	Calculation	Rate (mL O_2/minute)
Germinating Peas 10°C	0.12 mL/20 min = 0.006	0.006 mL/min
Germinating Peas 30°C	0.27 mL/20 min = 0.14	0.14 mL/min
Dry Peas and Beads 10°C	0 mL/20 min = 0	0 mL/min
Dry Peas and Beads 30°C	0 mL/20 min = 0	0 mL/min

Lab 6   Molecular Biology

Exercise 6A: Bacterial Transformation—
Ampicillin Resistance

Plate Number	Condition	Observation
1	LB with transformed plasmid (positive control)	Lawn
2	LB w/o transformed plasmid (negative control)	Lawn
3	LB/Amp with transformed plasmid (experimental)	50 colonies
4	LB/Amp w/o transformed plasmid (positive control)	None

- Interpretation of this exercise:

  ➤ Plate numbers 1 and 2 will have lawns of bacteria because there was no antibiotic in the plate.

  ➤ Plate number 3 had 50 transformed colonies because some of the cells were transformed with the plasmids containing the gene for resistance to ampicillin.

  ➤ Plate number 4 has no colonies since no plasmid was transformed and the bacteria are susceptible to ampicillin.

  ➤ Transformation Efficiency is calculated in the following way (hypothetical calculation):

  $$\text{Total mass of plasmid used} = \frac{0.0075 \ g}{L} \times 20 \ L = 0.15 \ g$$

  Total volume of cell suspension = 500µL

  $$\text{Mass of plasmidin suspension} = \frac{100\mu L}{500\mu L} = .2 \times 0.15\mu g = 0.03\mu g$$

  $$\text{Number of colonies per } g \text{ of plasmid} = \frac{50 \text{ colonies}}{0.03 \ g}$$

  $$= \frac{1.67 \times 10^3 \text{ colonies}}{g}$$

Exercise 6B: Restriction Enzyme Cleavage of DNA and Electrophoresis

Hind III

Actual bp	Measured Distance in cm
21,130	3.0
9,416	3.9
6,557	4.8
4,361	6.1
2,322	9.1
2,027	9.6
570	Cannot see on gel
125	Cannot see on gel

EcoR1

Band	Measured Distance in cm	Actual bp	Interpolated bp from Graph
1	2.8	21,226	19,000
2	4.4	7,421	9,000
3	4.9	5,804	7,000
4	5.1	5,643	6,800
5	5.7	4,878	5,000
6	6.9	3,530	4,300

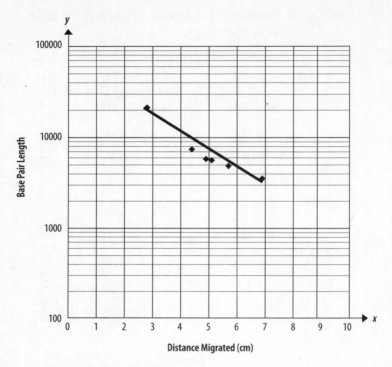

Distance Migrated (cm)

- Interpretation of this exercise:

  ➤ Lambda phage DNA was incubated with restriction enzymes HindIII and EcoR1 separately. The migration distance of the DNA bands produced by Hind III were measured in centimeters and were plotted against base pair size using semi-log paper. This was accomplished with DNA gel electrophoresis.

  ➤ Drawing the line of best fit allows for interpolation of the same DNA cut with EcoR1. Based on the line of best fit, the base pair sizes of the lambda DNA can be found and compared to the known value.

- Important points of this laboratory include:

  ➤ Smaller pieces of DNA migrated faster and therefore are farther on the gel.

  ➤ The electrical current running through the buffer separate the DNA based on size. DNA is negatively charged; therefore, it migrates toward the positive end.

➤ If the restriction enzymes recognition site is mutated, the enzyme will not cut the DNA properly. The result will be the incorrect number and size of bands on the gel.

Lab 7 Genetics of Organisms

[*Note:* Most AP Biology teachers do not have their students carry out the 4–6 week experiment on the mating of *Drosophila melanogaster*. Unfortunately, this is a required AP laboratory so you need to be ready to answer questions about this lab.]

Part 1 The Life Cycle of *Drosophila*

1. *Eggs*—small and oval shaped, and usually found on the side of culture tube.
2. *Larval Stage*—wormlike stage that tunnel through the medium.
3. *Pupal Stage*—fully mature larva are called pupa and tend to be brown in color. Basic body parts can be observed.
4. *Adult Stage*—fly emerges from pupal casing and mating can take place again.

Part 2 Crosses

- Cross 1 monohybrid

  ➤ Assume normal wings is dominant to dumpy wings. Cross a pure breeding long wing (w^+) to a dumpy wing (w).

  F_1 Cross—w^+w^+ X ww → All progeny w^+w (all normal wings heterozygotes)

  F_2 Cross—w^+w X w^+w → Progeny *1 w^+ w^+:2 w^+w:1ww* (3 normal wings:1 short wing)

- Cross 2 dihybrid

  ➤ Assume gray body color (g^+) and normal wings (w^+) is dominant to black body color (g) and dumpy wings (w). Cross a pure breeding gray and normal wing to black and dumpy wing.

F$_1$ Cross—g^+ g^+w^+ w^+ X $ggww$ → All progeny g^+g w^+ w (all gray long wings heterozygotes)

F$_2$ Cross—g^+g w^+w X g^+g w^+w → Progeny g^+g w^+ w, $ggww$, g^+g ww, gg w^+ w

(1:1:1:1 gray, normal wings; black, dumpy wings; gray, dumpy wings; black, normal wings)

- Cross 3 sex-linked

  ➤ Eye color is sex-linked in *Drosophila melanogaster*. Assume red eye (X^{w+}) is dominant to white eye (X^w). Cross pure breeding red eye female to a white eye male.

  F$_1$ Cross—X^{w+} X^{w+} x X^wY → All progeny red eye: females are carriers X^{w+} X^w and male $X^{w+}Y$

  F$_2$ Cross—X^{w+} X^w x $X^{w+}Y$ → Progeny 1 X^{w+} X^w, 1 X^{w+} X^{w+}, 1 X^wY, 1 $X^{w+}Y$ (all females have red eyes, ½ males have red eyes, and ½ males have white eyes)

Part 3 Chi-square Analysis

- Chi square is a statistical test to insure the validity of a hypothesis.

  ➤ Null Hypothesis—there is no statistical difference between expected data and observed data.

  ➤ Alternative Hypothesis—another hypothesis that explains your observation.

- Formula is $X^2 = \sum \dfrac{(o-e)^2}{e}$

  o = observed number of individuals

  e = expected number of individuals

  Σ = sum of values

  Degrees of freedom = expected phenotypes −1

Use of the Chi Square Table of Critical Values

Probability (p)	Degrees of Freedom				
	1	2	3	4	5
0.05	3.84	5.99	7.82	9.49	11.1

If the calculated chi-square is greater than or equal to the critical value, the null hypothesis is rejected with a reassurance of 95%, meaning only 5% of the time would you see the null hypothesis as being correct.

Sample Data

Pheno-type	# Observed	# Expected	$(o-e)$	$(o-e)^2$	$(o-e)^2/e$
Normal wing	70	75	−5	25	0.33
Dumpy wing	30	25	5	25	1.00
				$X^2 = \sum \dfrac{(o-e)^2}{e}$	1.33

Result: There is no difference between observed and expected phenotypes; accept the null hypothesis.

Lab 8   Population Genetics

Exercise 8A: Estimating Allele Frequencies for a Specific Trait within a Sample Population

	Phenotypes		Allele Frequency Based on Hardy-Weinberg	
	Tasters $p^2 + 2pq$	Nontasters q^2	p	q
Class	40%	60%	$1 - .77 = 0.23$	$\sqrt{.60} = 0.77$
North America	55%	45%	$1 - .67 = 0.33$	$\sqrt{.45} = 0.67$

Class-Percent of $p^2 = (0.23)^2 - 5.0\%$

Class-Percent of $2pq = 2(.23)(.77) = 35\%$

Class-Percent of $q^2 = 60\%$ (*observed*)

- The interpretation of this exercise:

  ➤ This was an exercise to test the ability to assimilate the Hardy-Weinberg equation. The key point was to be able to take the square root of nontasters (recessive phenotype) in order to find the allele frequency of q.

Exercise 8B: Case Studies

CASE I—A Test of Ideal Hardy-Weinberg

- The interpretation of this exercise:

  ➤ A population that is in an Ideal Hardy-Weinberg would be a population of heterozygote individuals that follow all 5 key Hardy-Weinberg criteria:

    ✦ No mutation

    ✦ No gene flow or genetic variation

    ✦ A very large population sample

    ✦ No natural selection

    ✦ Random mating

Frequency of p and $q = 0.5$
Percent of $p^2 = 25\%$
Percent of $2pq = 50\%$
Percent of $q^2 = 25\%$

CASE II—Selection

- The interpretation of this exercise:

  ➤ Unlike CASE I, in this portion of the laboratory exercise a selection took place. Homozygous recessive (aa) individuals will not reproduce in this exercise thus not following the Ideal Hardy-Weinberg population.

  Frequency of $p = .8$ and $q = 0.2$
  Percent of $p^2 = 64\%$
  Percent of $2pq = 32\%$
  Percent of $q^2 = 4\%$

CASE III—Heterozygote Advantage

- The interpretation of this exercise:

  ➤ Unlike CASE I in this portion of the laboratory exercise a Heterozygote Advantage took place. Heterozygous individuals have a higher relative rate of productive success than either the homozygote dominant or homozygote recessive genotype.

  Frequency of $p = .65$ and $q = 0.35$
  Percent of $p^2 = 42\%$
  Percent of $2pq = 46\%$
  Percent of $q^2 = 12\%$

Lab 9   Transpiration

Exercise 9A: Transpiration

- The interpretation of this exercise:

  ➤ Transpiration or the uptake of water from the leaf surface is highest with both light and fan conditions. Both of these conditions cause water to be lost from the leaf surface. A water potential is created between the air surrounding the leaf and the potometer where the bottom of the stem contains water. Water will travel from an area of higher water potential to lower water potential. The mist condition mimics increased humidity, decreasing the water potential difference, since more water is occupying the surrounding air. The mist line is actually below that of the control (room) indicating the surrounding air has more water associated with it.

Cumulative Water Loss in mL/m²

	Time (minutes)			
Treatment	0	10	20	30
Room	0	1.50	3.20	4.7
Light	0	4.00	8.12	12.13
Fan	0	4.21	8.45	12.30
Mist	0	1.50	2.00	2.33

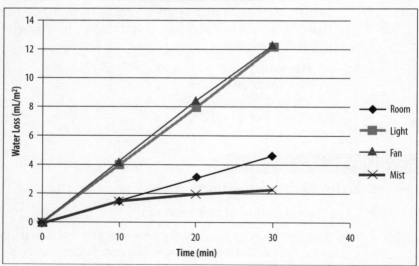

Water Loss vs. Time

Lab 10   Physiology of the Circulatory System

Exercise 10A: Measuring Blood Pressure

- The interpretation of this exercise:
  - ➤ Blood pressure is a measure of the amount of force on blood vessels. Systolic pressure is peak pressure in the arteries when the ventricles are contracting. Diastolic pressure is minimum pressure in the arteries, when the ventricles are filled with blood. The ratio of systolic and diastolic pressure is the measurement of blood pressure.

Exercise 10B: A Test of Fitness

- The interpretation of this exercise:
  - ➤ The heart rate and blood pressure of a person rises when moving from a lying-down position to a standing position.

Exercise 10C: Heart Rate and Temperature

- The interpretation of this exercise:
  - ➤ Daphnia are small crustaceans that live in a multitude of different aquatic environments. Daphnia are also ectothermic (cold-blooded) animals that regulate their body temperatures via the heat exchange from the outside environment. For example, they may bask in the sun to warm up or crawl under a rock to cool down. In this exercise Daphnia were exposed to different water temperatures, and heart rate was measured by counting the number of beats per minute. The relationship below is linear, indicating the environment temperature does regulate the heart rate (increase) of daphnia.

Reading	Temperature (°C)	Heart Rate (beats/min)
1	10°C	50
2	15°C	60
3	20°C	70
4	25°C	80
5	30°C	90
6	35°C	100
7	40°C	110
8	45°C	120

Heart Rate vs. Temperature

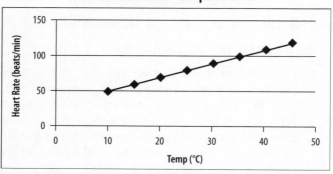

Lab 11   Animal Behavior

Exercise 11A: General Observations of Behaviors

- The interpretation of this exercise:

  ➤ Pillbugs are terrestrial isopods that are members of the Phylum Arthropoda and Class Crustacea. When given the choice between a dry or wet chamber, they tend to gravitate toward the moist environment. This is because pillbugs lack a cuticle on their outside portion and lose moisture rather easily.

Number of Pillbugs vs. Time

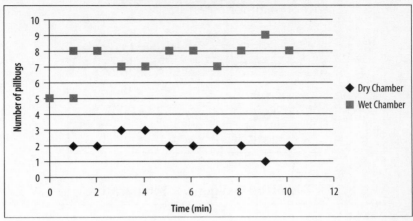

Exercise 11B: Reproductive Behavior in Fruit Flies

- The interpretation of this exercise:
  - ➤ Many organisms exhibit behaviors that indicate courtship. For *Drosophila melanogaster* a list of male and female characteristics are listed below:
    - ✦ Male (tend to exhibit behaviors that promote mating): stamping the forefeet, circling the female, and wing vibration.
    - ✦ Female (tend to exhibit behaviors that do not promote mating): ignoring, depressing wings, or flying.

Lab 12   Dissolved Oxygen and Aquatic Primary

Exercise 12A: Dissolved Oxygen and Temperature

- The interpretation of this exercise:
  - ➤ The amount of dissolved oxygen decreases as the temperature increases, indicating the amount of oxygen available for respiration depends on temperature. Biological processes such as photosynthesis increase the concentration of oxygen in water while aerobic respiration decreases cellular respiration. The measurement of dissolved oxygen is

an important factor in determining the fitness of an aquatic environment for organisms.

Temperature	Dissolved Oxygen (mg/mL)
5°C	2.0
15°C	1.5
25°C	1.2

Dissolved Oxygen vs. Temperature

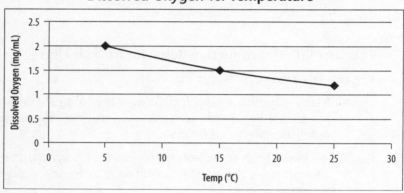

Exercise 12B: A Model of Productivity as a Function of Depth in a Lake

- The interpretation of this exercise:

  ➤ *Primary Productivity*—the amount of light energy converted to chemical energy in an ecosystem, by autotrophic organisms.

  ➤ *Gross Primary Productivity*—total primary productivity.

  ➤ *Net Primary Productivity*—the energy used by producers for cellular respiration subtracted from the gross primary productivity.

➤ The screens in the experiment mimic depth of a lake. As the number of screens increase, the amount of light decreases, as well as gross and primary productivity. As the amount of light decreases, the rate of photosynthesis decreases (productivity) because the light drives the photosynthetic reactions.

# of screens	% light	Gross Productivity	Net Productivity
0	100	0.13	0.04
1	65	0.13	0.04
3	25	0.10	0.01
5	10	0.08	-0.02
8	2	0.06	-0.03

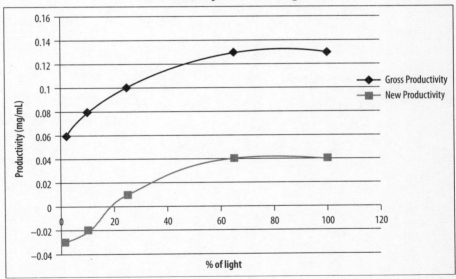

Productivity vs. % of Light

Essay Writing—Exemplars, Data Analysis/ Graphing Techniques, Setting Up an Experiment

Below are some guidelines that you must adhere to when answering free-response questions on the AP Biology exam.

- All answers must be in essay form—outlines will not earn you any points.

- Drawing diagrams is an effective way to augment your essay. Remember a diagram alone will not be enough to earn any points. You must link it to your essay answer.

- When in doubt, write, write, write! AP essays are scored on the ability to gain points, and not based on losing points.

Do not be surprised if you are required to graph data for one of the four free-response questions. There are simple rules to use to achieve maximum points for this portion of your essay. Like many things on the AP test, just follow the rules that govern the test and you will be fine.

A. Graph Setup and Plotting (usually worth 2–3 points on the scoring rubric)

Rule 1: Make sure you have a title for your graph. Your title must be informative for the reader to grant you maximum points. A good way to make sure you have a good title is to name the graph based on the y (dependent axis) and x (independent axis).

Rule 2: The independent axis of any graph is the horizontal x-axis. Always graph time on the independent axis. It is one of the AP's favorite independent variables along with temperature. Label the independent axis not only with time or temperature, but with units required (seconds, minutes, hours, or degrees Celsius).

The dependent axis is graphed on the vertical *y*-axis. The dependent axis represents what you are measuring such as growth, amount of substrate used, percent increase or decrease.

Here is an example:

Day 1	Day 2	Day 3	Day 4	Day 5
2 cm	4 cm	6 cm	8 cm	10 cm

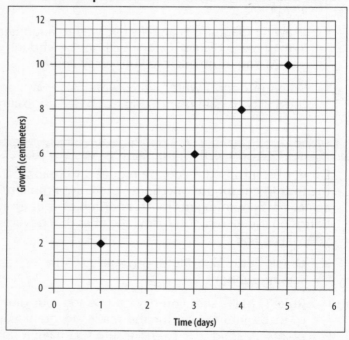

Relationship Between Growth of Plant and Time

Notice that the intervals between the units are equally marked for both time and growth. This needs to be based on the experimental data that is given to you in the question. The coordinate system you will be given on the test will be framed and you must work within the parameters of that framed graph.

B. Using the Graph to Answer Further Questions (usually worth 3–4 points on the scoring rubric)

Once your data is plotted, you will have to use it to correctly answer a series of questions from the plot. These answers can range from quick mathematical calculations involving slope or simple extrapolations of the data based on trends.

Slope Calculation:

➤ The mathematical formula for slope is: $m = \dfrac{\Delta y}{\Delta x} = \dfrac{y_2 - y_1}{x_2 - x_1}$, and indicates the rise of a line divided by its run. Taking a look at this graph below we can determine the slope, or rate of oxygen produced per minute, via the formula.

➤ Simply pick two points on the line and the corresponding x and y coordinates.

➤ $m = \dfrac{y_2 - y_1}{x_2 - x_1} = \dfrac{10 \text{ cm} - 2 \text{ cm}}{5 \text{ days} - 1 \text{ day}} = \dfrac{8 \text{ cm}}{4 \text{ days}} = 2 \text{ cm/day}$

➤ The interpretation from the graph is that the plant will grow 2 cm per day.

Relationship Between Growth of Plant and Time

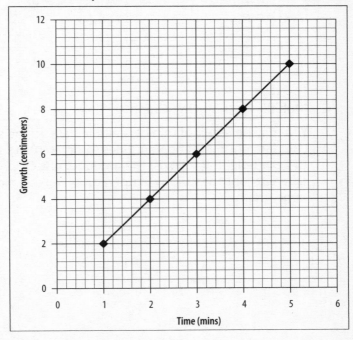

Extrapolation:

➤ Data that is graphed correctly can be used to make an extrapolation, or produce expected data points from a set of known points on a graph. All data on AP tests show a trend that can be used in extrapolation. The best method to indicate extrapolation is to use a dotted line to show where the data has been expanded.

➤ Question: Using the graph below, determine how much oxygen gas is consumed at 5 minutes.

Relation Between Amount of O_2 Consumed and Time

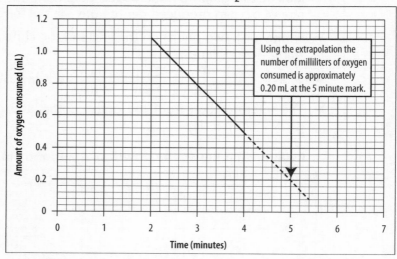

C. Multiple Plots on One Graph

You may be required to plot multiple data on the same graph. Use different marks on your lines to differentiate the plots. In the example that follows, the amounts of CO_2 produced in 3 different tubes at various temperatures were all plotted on the same graph.

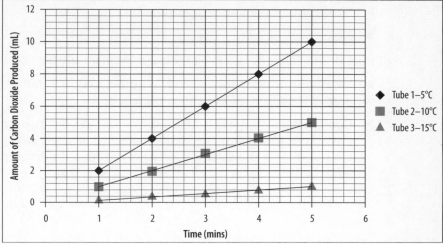

Relation of Amount of CO$_2$ Produced and Time

Part 3   Setting Up an Experiment

Free-response questions on the AP Biology test may require you to design an experiment to test the effects of a certain condition on a measurement. For example, you could be asked to design an experiment that measures the effects of pH on the activity of an enzyme such as catalase. To maximize your earned points, follow these simple rules:

- **Rule 1:** Identify the independent and dependent variables and the experimental constants.

  ➤ Independent: pH changes (3–11)

  ➤ Dependent: Measurement of catalase activity

  ➤ Constant: Temperature will remain the same as well as the amount of catalase being used in the experiment.

- **Rule 2:** Make a hypothesis.

  ➤ The catalase enzyme has an optimal pH in which it will have maximum activity. Making a prediction is required when setting up an experiment.

- **Rule 3:** Indicate a control(s).
  - ➤ No enzyme or denatured enzyme.
  - ➤ Neutral pH of 7.
- **Rule 4:** Indicate how you will measure the data produced.
  - ➤ Measuring the amount of oxygen produced or hydrogen peroxide consumed at various pH levels.
  - ➤ Construction of a graph that indicates what your hypothesis states. Indicating the multiple trials and repeatability are essential in the scientific process to prove the hypothesis.

Notes

Notes

Notes

Notes

Notes

Notes

Notes

Notes